"With heartbreaking detail, Roberts courageously tells how God's grace transformed her unspeakable pain into love and forgiveness. Caution advised: You won't be able to put this book down once you start reading."

—Donald B. Kraybill, author of *Amish Grace*

Forgiven

The Amish School Shooting,

a Mother's Love,

and a Story of Remarkable Grace

TERRI ROBERTS
with Jeanette Windle

BETHANY HOUSE PUBLISHERS
a division of Baker Publishing Group
Minneapolis, Minnesota

© 2015 by Terri Roberts

Published by Bethany House Publishers
11400 Hampshire Avenue South
Bloomington, Minnesota 55438
www.bethanyhouse.com

Bethany House Publishers is a division of
Baker Publishing Group, Grand Rapids, Michigan

Printed in the United States of America

Library of Congress Cataloging-in-Publication Data
Roberts, Terri.
    Forgiven : the Amish school shooting, a mother's love, and a story of
remarkable grace / Terri Roberts, with Jeanette Windle.
        pages cm
        Summary: "The mother of the man who shot many young Amish
    schoolgirls before taking his own life tells of the grace she's received from the
    Amish, the relationships she's built with the victims and their families, and the
    healing and forgiveness she's found"— Provided by publisher.
        ISBN 978-0-7642-1732-6 (pbk. : alk. paper)
        1. Forgiveness of sin. 2. Forgiveness—Religious aspects—Christianity.
    3. Amish School Shooting, Nickel Mines, Pa., 2006. 4. Roberts, Terri.
    5. Amish—Pennsylvania—Lancaster County. 6. Amish—Doctrines. I. Title.
    BT795.R58 2015
    289.774815—dc23   2015015646

Cover design by Paul Higdon and Dan Thornberg, Design Source
Creative Services

15   16   17   18   19   20   21   7   6   5   4   3   2   1

In keeping with biblical principles of
creation stewardship, Baker Publishing Group advocates the responsible
use of our natural resources. As a
member of the Green Press Initiative, our company uses recycled
paper when possible. The text paper
of this book is composed in part of
post-consumer waste.

May you find peace that passes understanding
through surrender and forgiveness as you absorb
the lessons these pages reveal to you.

———————◇◆◇———————

Seek

Joy Through Adversity

in the moment, with expectation!

Contents

Contents

Acknowledgments

I would like to express my love and appreciation to my husband, Chuck, and our family and friends who have been an integral part of this amazing journey in faith and healing. Because of you, we've been able to move forward in a healthy environment.

I am thankful to each and every one who has offered prayers and support, and I especially want to thank Cheri Lovre. Cheri has been an invaluable source of strength and direction as I navigated the muddy waters of healing. I am forever indebted to her for her willingness and ability to take the anxiety and emotion of the moment and help frame it in a way that gave options for navigating the next step. She has been God's special blessing to me as I waded through deep waters.

A special mention to all my Amish friends from the Nickel Mines community who have shown such great interest and concern for our lives in our ongoing, growing friendships. Amish names mentioned in this book are already of public record. These words are not intended to bring glory to the person, but to share how their lives have honored God through interactions I've had with them. All of the glory and honor goes to God the Father for the healing we have all experienced in this process.

Foreword

I still remember the outrage I felt as the news of the Lancaster County Amish schoolhouse shooting swept across media networks the morning of October 2, 2006. Within hours, ABC News and the Associated Press contacted me, wanting quotes. My Plain cousins, friends of two of the Amish families whose daughters were critically wounded, asked if I would request prayer from my readers for the peace-abiding people of Nickel Mines, Pennsylvania. Ultimately, as word reached beyond America's shores, prayers for the injured survivors, as well as for the families of the deceased, were being offered up all over the globe.

What also emerged was sheer astonishment as believers and unbelievers alike struggled to comprehend the Amish bishop's immediate offer of forgiveness to the family of Charlie Roberts, the shooter. "How can mercy be extended for such a crime?" some questioned. "How can you simply forgive, once and for all?" others wondered.

My knee-jerk response came as a simple reminder that each of us is called to forgive those who do us harm. What Christ taught in the Beatitudes is clear—if we want to be forgiven, we must extend forgiveness to others.

The bishop's pardon stirred up heated discussion about an all-encompassing forgiveness. Many had strong opinions; some even disputed how the Amish people could meekly follow their minister's lead in such an across-the-board act of mercy.

The families of the five little girls who died, as well as those with gravely wounded daughters, began to share that theirs was not merely a one-time offering of forgiveness. Rather, they had to purposefully *choose* to forgive daily and, in some cases, hour-by-hour. The father of one young victim who survived, but needs constant care, admitted that he often questions himself: *Have I truly forgiven?*

Author Terri Roberts' journey to wholeness is a striking testimony to the power of this amazing forgiveness. Shattered emotionally by her son's crime, she realized that she, too, must forgive him. Yet how does a mother move forward after such an unthinkable deed?

I wept at the author's travail over what she might have done that autumn morning, had she known, to thwart the tragedy to come. *Where was God that horrific day? Why didn't He step in and intervene?* My heart was also softened by the stories of the brokenhearted Amish families whose surrender to the sovereign will of our Lord became instrumental in the author's emotional healing.

This riveting account, written by a brave and brokenhearted mother, may not be what you're expecting. In fact, it may surprise you. But it will surely present you with an enduring hope that can only come from the loving hand of our heavenly Father. You will be drawn, as I was, to embrace fully the miracle and blessing of forgiveness.

—Beverly Lewis

Prologue

You have put me in the lowest pit, in the darkest depths.

—Psalm 88:6

Picture an idyllic, sun-kissed valley. Fields stretch to the base of a pine-cloaked ridge, a green and yellow patchwork of tall, tasseled corn, drying alfalfa, ripened wheat and barley. Apple and cherry orchards raise boughs heavy with ripening fruit. A creek, whose clear water offers refreshment on the hottest summer days to valley residents, both humans and animals, contributes trickling harmonies. And there is the laughter of children playing.

Let's not forget the laughter.

No valley is without storms. Rains, soft and hard, occasionally flatten crops, scatter flower petals and unripened fruit. But those same inconvenient rains provide the moisture that makes this sheltered paradise so fertile. Within the valley's memory there has even been a hurricane or two, ripping shingles from

13

roofs, toppling fences and trees, sweeping away chickens, and ripping crops from the earth. The farmhouse and barn survived these storms, having been built strong and on solid foundations. The valley, though not untouched, was quickly restored by picking up the broken pieces, replanting the lost crops.

And then one day a new and different storm arises. No mere hurricane this one, but a tsunami. There's been no warning. No single feather of a cloud in a blue autumn sky. Only the trembling of the earth underfoot. Against the merciless, impersonal awfulness of that monstrous curling wave, what use the desperate cries for mercy, for help? What can the valley do except brace for annihilation?

That serene, perfect valley is an image of my own life. Tucked away in my memory is a truly idyllic childhood. I was privileged to grow up amidst lush countryside, rolling hills, quiet woods, and quaint villages in one of our Creator's most perfect garden spots—Lancaster County in central Pennsylvania. I never doubted the love of parents, grandparents, siblings, aunts, uncles, cousins. Or the existence of a loving and good heavenly Father. I met and married a wonderful man who was—and still is—not only the love of my life but also my best friend. We were blessed with four beautiful, healthy sons.

Of course, life is never without its storms. The normal wind and rains of raising four rambunctious boys. A miscarriage. The inevitable ups and downs of marriage. The challenges of a demanding job. A hurricane blew in with a diagnosis of breast cancer. But I'd survived every challenge. Life was good. My children were grown and settled. I had grandchildren to love. Other mothers would approach me to say what a wonderful job I'd done raising four sons. My very identity was wrapped up in being a wife and mother who wanted God's best for each member of her family. I was living the "happily ever after."

Then the tsunami struck. On October 2, 2006, my firstborn child, whom I'd cradled in my arms, overseen his first steps, taught to love and serve God, watched grow into a gentle, hard-working man, a loving husband and father—this beloved son walked into an Amish schoolhouse with an arsenal of guns. Before it was over, five precious young girls were dead, five more were seriously injured, and my son had taken his own life.

Suddenly I had a new identity: the mother of the Amish schoolhouse shooter. I cannot describe my devastation, the gut-wrenching pain, the nights of anguish. All those sweet young lives, families, our own family—changed forever because of a single senseless act of evil and rage committed by my own dear son.

I would survive this tsunami. I found myself hanging on by my fingertips as the storm battered my body, inexorably loosening my feeble grip. What kind of a mother was I that my son could do such a terrible thing? Where was the God who'd been there with me in all the other storms of my life? The God in whom I'd taught my children to place their trust? Why had He not stopped this? Was there a single ray of light, of hope in this darkness?

I could not see the light. I could not hold on. But even as I found myself swept away by this rogue tsunami wave, in the darkest depths of my pain, I felt loving arms enfold me. And in surrendering to that sweet embrace, I was reminded that survival is not the only word that starts with the letter *s*. It is in *surrender* that I found balm for my pain. Surrender to the One who had been with me through every storm and who had not abandoned me in this one.

We live in a society that glorifies survival. That teaches us to seek revenge when wronged, to come out on top. I had braced myself for the inevitable hate and vengeance. Instead, I encountered love beyond understanding. Forgiveness from the very Amish families whose daughters my son had swept from their arms. And I discovered by their example that submission and surrender, love and forgiveness are not weaknesses, but the strength our world so desperately needs.

Ongoing interaction with the Amish community has profoundly touched and changed my life. Together with them, I've found release from bitterness, anger, and fear in mutual forgiveness and love. It hasn't been an easy journey. But step by step, one day at a time, I've found the strength to move forward. To *love* forward.

In my reflections over time, I am in awe of how the Lord has provided opportunities for me to praise Him when in the natural I should be sorrowful. All these years later, I find myself in a "spacious place" that I can barely explain (Psalm 18:19). Today I write these words sitting in my sun-room, a gift from a compassionate Amish builder, drinking in the calm serenity, listening to the birds singing, enjoying a soft breeze on my face. And I marvel at this realm of peace that has come only through surrender and letting God fill the dark recesses of my heart.

I write this book so that others, too, may experience the peace that passes understanding, and hope for their future. That others living with anger, unforgiveness, and bitterness may discover, as I have, the power and the gift of freedom that forgiveness offers. I invite you to come with me on my journey of faith into an unfathomable abyss—a darkness too deep for the human spirit to encompass. Share my journey into healing, one step at a time.

May this day be the beginning of your own journey.

1

The Happening

I am confined and cannot escape; my eyes are dim with grief.

—Psalm 88:8–9

It was good to be home.

The last two weeks had been an exciting adventure of serving God in Toulouse, France. In September 2006, our church had organized a work team to help restore a ministry center that was reaching inner-city youth and refugees in the heart of southern France. While there I'd helped with yard work, painting, and other restoration projects. As a break from our labor, our hosts had taken the team on a tour of Europe's oldest remaining walled city, Carcassonne, where parts of the Kevin Costner movie *Robin Hood* was filmed.

I left France excited and filled with stories to tell. I was also glad to be going home. On the drive from the airport, I was reminded afresh that of all the places I'd visited, none was more beautiful than Lancaster County. Our own home was just south of the small town of Strasburg, a few miles from Lancaster City. The historic railroad capital of Pennsylvania, Strasburg is a quaint tourist center with railroad and model train museums, an antique railway, and countless small shops and other attractions. Among these is the famed Sight & Sound Theatre, a two-thousand-seat complex built in the middle of a cornfield where Broadway-quality musical productions of biblical stories such as *Joseph*, *Moses*, *Jonah*, and *Miracle of Christmas* draw visitors from around the world.

The countryside around Strasburg is farmed by the Amish, a Pennsylvania Dutch subculture that combines devout Christian faith with a simple lifestyle that has changed little since the sixteenth century. About thirty thousand Amish live in Lancaster County. Once I'd left the main highway, my drive home passed through countryside dotted with neat farmhouses and barns. Black trousers, blue shirts and dresses, and white aprons flapping on clotheslines were a reminder that these families lived without washers and dryers.

The end of September is harvesttime in Lancaster County. Out in the fields, Amish farmers were piling cut cornstalks onto wagons. Yellow squash and orange pumpkins dotted the fields. Dried tobacco leaves and hay were being bundled for market. I shared the road with horse-drawn buggies and Amish youth heading home from school on foot-pedaled scooters.

My husband, Chuck, and I lived only two miles from the Strasburg town center, but the quiet country lane offered the feeling of unspoiled countryside. Our home had been built on a four-acre lot purchased from an Amish farmer, Jake Stoltzfoos. His son Henry was our nearest neighbor, while Henry's brother Chris owned the field adjacent to our property. Other than these neighbors, I'd had little personal contact with the Amish community. But my husband, a retired police officer, ran a chauffeur service for the Amish needing transportation beyond driving range of their buggies and wagons. He'd recently purchased a van for this purpose. On either side were magnetic signs with Chuck's name and phone number advertising his service to potential customers.

A few other non-Amish houses shared our lane. Beyond the houses rose a ridge thick with pine and deciduous trees. During my time in France, the leaves had begun turning to the rich red, orange, and gold hues of fall. As I arrived home, the air was crisp and tangy, and I remember thinking how beautiful the fall colors were, and whether a sunset over a medieval French city or southern European beach could be any more beautiful than one over the rolling fields and hills of my home.

The evening of October 1 was my first opportunity to share my trip with family. Our second son, Josh, was in Louisiana working on a reconstruction project in the aftermath of Hurricane Katrina, and our third son, Zach, was living in Manhattan. Our youngest son, Jon, and his wife, Megan, already had plans that Sunday evening. But I was delighted that my oldest son, Charlie, along with his wife, Marie, and their three children could join us. Their oldest daughter had just turned seven. Her younger brothers were five years old and eighteen months.

It seemed forever since I'd seen them last before leaving for France, and I hugged all three grandchildren, enjoying some good grandma moments. When we were finished eating and sharing about the trip, Charlie took his older son outside to play softball. Marie and I chatted at the breakfast bar. Their tenth wedding anniversary would be coming up in just a few weeks, and Charlie's thirty-third birthday not long after in early December.

Another exciting topic of discussion was my next major project for the upcoming winter months. My dream room had begun to take shape in my mind about three years earlier as I pondered where my husband and I were at this stage in our lives. Our children were grown, and the two of us were heading into our retirement years. I wanted to create a sanctuary where we could find peace and quiet, rest and reflection.

What brings revitalization and joy for me is when the sun is visible or directly shining on me. We decided on a sun-room, so I'd begun planning and saving for it. There were countless possibilities. It would be a wonderful place of tranquility and a delightful place to exercise and entertain. Once I'd rested from the France trip and the fall calendar settled into a routine, we would arrange with the contractor to begin.

A short while later, Charlie and his son came back inside, and the house began to empty out. It had been a good evening. I remember thinking as we all said our farewells that Charlie had seemed quieter than usual. He was an introvert by personality and never one to talk a lot in a group situation. Would it have made a difference, I asked myself later, if I'd made a point to ask him how he was doing? Would he have opened up to me? Changed what he was thinking? Changed his plans? Waving good-bye to Charlie, Marie, and the children, I could not have conceived it would be the last time I'd see my son alive.

The next morning I got up early. Sunrise was as beautiful above the fields surrounding our house as the previous night's sunset. Completing my normal routine of devotional reading and prayer, followed by exercise, I headed into work. I had been employed for the past thirteen years at Sight & Sound Theatre and was now manager for concessions and sales items, a position that offered challenges, but a job I loved. The sun shone bright as I drove through Strasburg to the huge theatre complex just up the road. The temperature was perfect for a gorgeous fall day. I felt no sense of foreboding, no darkness of spirit.

After a busy morning, I was glad to join a good friend and co-worker, Delores, for lunch out on the patio. Delores and I were enjoying relaxed conversation when I heard sirens in the distance. Helicopters sped by overhead. What could possibly be happening in this quiet rural community? As always when I hear emergency sirens, I offered a short prayer for whoever was in need and for the first responders involved, then went back to our conversation. When lunch ended, I returned to my office. As I stepped inside, the telephone was ringing. I picked it up. The caller was my husband. He asked me to come immediately to our son Charlie's home.

He went into no detail. But as I hurried down the stairway from my office, that foreboding I hadn't felt earlier began squeezing at my stomach, and a sense of urgency quickened my steps. It would take something very important for my husband to call me away from work.

The drive to Charlie and Marie's home took only ten minutes. I turned on the radio. A news story was unfolding. There had been a shooting at an Amish schoolhouse in nearby Nickel Mines, Bart Township. Children were among the dead and injured. The reported perpetrator's name was Roy (an incorrect reporting, I would find out a short time later).

Immediately my thoughts and heart began to race. My son Charlie drove a tanker truck for his father-in-law's business, which collected milk for processing every night from area dairy farms, many of them Amish. Charlie often parked his milk truck right near the school. Could he have somehow seen what the shooter was attempting, tried to intervene, and been shot? What if he'd been killed? Was that why my husband had called? Had he been vague so I wouldn't be driving while upset?

My stomach was churning as tumultuously as my thoughts by the time I pulled into our son's driveway. A state trooper and my husband were standing in the yard as I stepped out of the car. With fear clutching at my heart, I walked right up to the trooper and asked if my son was alive.

"No, ma'am," he responded somberly.

I turned to my husband. With deep pain in his eyes, he choked out, "It was Charlie. He killed those girls."

2

Tsunami!

But I cry to you for help, LORD; in the morning my prayer comes before you.

—Psalm 88:13

Our son had not only died, but was also the perpetrator of this heinous crime? My head throbbed with hot, searing pain as I tried to grapple with this news. No, this could not be! Not our wonderful son, the man of whom we'd always had reason to be proud. He'd never committed a crime in his life, never even been in any serious trouble. He was a loving son, husband, and father. He had a wonderful wife and three beautiful children. There had to be some mistake!

And what about the radio news coverage of a perpetrator named Roy? I seized on that. It had been confirmed that the crime was carried out by someone else. The trooper must have missed the update. It was surely all just a mix-up.

But already that small hope was being swept away. The trooper's terse, unvarnished narrative was too raw, too terrible to be denied. The details were a jumble my anguished mind could not take in, but I grasped that Charlie had called our daughter-in-law Marie before taking his life and the others'. He'd even left suicide notes saying good-bye to his family.

We didn't learn all the particulars at this time. But eventually we would find out that Charlie and Marie had seen their two older children off on the school bus as usual that morning. Charlie had then supposedly left for a work appointment while Marie took her youngest son to a prayer group she led for mothers of young children at a nearby church.

But Charlie had not gone to a work appointment. He'd driven a borrowed pickup to an intersection near the Nickel Mines schoolhouse, where he'd parked so often before. He waited until the children finished their morning recess. Then he backed his vehicle up to the schoolhouse steps and unloaded an arsenal of guns we hadn't even known he possessed, along with tools, boards, and other items.

When he made an excuse to gain access into the unlocked schoolroom, there was no resistance from the twenty-year-old teacher and twenty-three students, some of whom recognized him as the driver who collected milk from their families' dairy farms each night. Once inside, he'd produced a pistol and ordered all male students outside, along with the teacher, her sixteen-year-old sister, her two sisters-in-law, and her mother. The remaining ten girls ranged in age from six to thirteen. Immobilizing them with plastic zip ties, he'd then used his tools to secure boards over the windows and door so escape or rescue was impossible.

But by then the teacher and male students had already run for help. State troopers and other law enforcement arrived on the scene within minutes. Had Charlie not even considered this likelihood? Had he wanted to be caught?

It was during this time lapse that Charlie called his wife. By now a law enforcement bullhorn was demanding Charlie's surrender. He answered with a shotgun blast and then turned his weapons execution style on the girls. By the time state troopers had smashed their way through the barricades, he'd turned a pistol on himself.

Two older girls and one six-year-old girl died immediately. Did they suffer? I can only pray not. Two more were airlifted to emergency rooms but did not make it. Five still lived and were by this time being rushed into surgery at three different area hospitals. My heart broke at the thought of those poor little girls! And more so at what their parents must be going through.

Darkness and anguish were overwhelming me so that I could not breathe. My husband's eyes, full of grief and pain, confirmed to me this was no nightmare from which I would awake. I recall falling to the ground in a fetal position, wailing as though to expel the built-up agony and horror. Someone came from the house, asking for quiet. My eighteen-month-old grandson was sleeping.

If I was devastated, how terrible this must be for Marie, Charlie's wonderful wife. I somehow forced my body to stand, and with my husband, Chuck, and the state trooper, we entered our son's house. My sweet daughter-in-law had already suffered the initial shock and was far more composed than I was. She told us what she knew of the morning's events, her phone conversation with Charlie, and the notes he'd left.

But her focus was on her children and how she could shield them from the media circus soon to gather outside the house. The decision had been made for Marie and the children to go to her parents' home a block away. The two oldest were still at school, unaware that their peaceful, loving universe had just been ripped apart. Marie's mother had arrived and was helping Marie pack up clothing and other essential items.

I tried to be helpful but those next hours are only a blur in my mind. I remember feeling hollow inside and in desperate need of water. My mouth was so parched that it was a struggle to speak. I asked the trooper for a glass of water, then another and another, but nothing seemed to help.

During this time, there were more police in the house, searching through closets and drawers, rummaging under furniture. Looking for guns, I would guess, or any indication as to why Charlie would have done such a thing. At some point, state troopers left with my husband to drive to our house. I found out later they wanted to check our gun safe for any weapons that might have belonged to Charlie. My husband had been a police officer for thirty years, a man of honorable standing in the community. I could not imagine his feelings as he was escorted out to the police cruiser like a perpetrator after thirty years of being the one who did the escorting.

On the drive, the state trooper pulled over to deal with a phone call. While he did so, Chuck called my niece Melissa, who lived nearby, and asked her to pull the magnetic signs from his Amish taxi. This was not a time to have the name *Roberts* on the side of a vehicle dedicated to the Amish community.

By this time Marie's mother had gone to pick up the children at school. Not knowing what else to do, I noticed Dale, Charlie's five-year-old yellow Labrador, running around. He wouldn't be able to accompany Marie and the children to her parents' house, so I offered to take him home. When I asked for his leash, it couldn't be found. Perhaps it had been left with Grandma and Grandpa.

Marie's grandparents lived next door, so I walked over to ask for the dog's leash. As they dug around to find it, I saw that the TV was on in the background. The news story was clearly of the schoolhouse shooting. I didn't know how much they knew of what had happened or of Charlie's responsibility in the situation, but I could not bring myself to ask them. My thoughts went to my own parents, with whom I had not yet had the opportunity to speak. To find out such news through the media would be too much for them to bear.

Marie's grandparents quickly turned up the leash, and I took it and hurried back to Charlie's house. Chuck had returned with the state trooper, and he loaded the dog into his own vehicle and headed for home.

By now everyone was gathering at the home of Marie's parents, Ken and Nadine Welk, who lived just a block away, and they asked me to join them. Nadine soon arrived with Marie and Charlie's older children. They weren't yet aware of what had happened, and we all did our best to maintain some semblance of normalcy for their sakes. I recall being encouraged to help my oldest granddaughter with her homework. I sat down with her and tried to concentrate on the lesson but could not focus my mind.

Above all, I was preoccupied with my own parents, Baba and Pop Pop, finding out about Charlie's involvement in the tragedy on the news. I finally excused myself and headed to their house. The TV was on in the living room. I will never forget the anguish on my dear mother's face or my father's expression of such disbelief and sorrow.

Tears streamed down my face as my mother and I embraced. We had spent so much time in prayer for our children and grandchildren. The oldest of all their grandchildren, Charlie had been so dearly loved by my parents and had brought so much joy to them over the years. We could not make sense of this. We could only hold each other and weep.

When I finally returned home, Chuck was there with Charlie's dog. I had not seen my strong, protective ex-police-officer husband shed tears since his father passed away many years before. Now he could not even lift his head. He'd covered his face with a dish towel to control the flow of tears. His eyes were sunken and dull, his face red, his forehead raw from wiping it with the towel.

Between deep, heartrending sobs, he kept repeating: "All those poor people. Those poor, poor children. Those poor mothers. Those poor fathers. Those poor grandparents. My poor, poor son. My baby son. I wish I would have been a better dad."

Before long more law enforcement showed up. Three detectives went with Chuck into the front room. Two more took me aside to question me about Charlie, seeking clues as to why this had happened.

But I had no answers, only questions. Even with incontrovertible evidence, I still struggled to accept the reality of the day's events. My son had grown up so loved—and loving. He had a wonderful wife, three beautiful children, a job he had aspired to and attained. Nothing of the bizarre, horrific, *evil* decisions he'd made this day matched the man I knew.

I struggled to give coherent responses. At times I would simply break down and cry. They finally left. The sun was setting over the fields that were visible from our back patio, gold and green and orange with their harvest bounty. The Amish harvest crews had left their work as word spread of the tragedy. As I stood on the patio, my desire for a sun-room, a sanctuary of peace designed to give glory to my heavenly Father, seemed a foolish, childish dream.

Where were you, God? I found myself screaming out mentally. *You knew what Charlie was going to do. You could have stopped him. You could have made his car get a flat tire. How could you let this happen? How could you let evil win?*

Anger was now warring with my pain and disbelief. Not just at God or even the circumstances. I was so angry at Charlie. Angry that his wrong actions could make his father, my wonderful, kind husband, blame himself, doubt himself as a parent and as a man. And Marie and the children. How could he do this to them? Leave his wife a widow, his children fatherless? Leave them to face the shame and the horror? And the gentle Amish families he'd come to know so well in his rounds collecting milk. What darkness and evil could so possess his mind that he would want to hurt them? To rip away daughters as precious as his own? To inflict such pain and loss on another living soul?

Dale seemed so confused and nervous, nosing around for his master and family. The yellow Lab was a beloved family pet, my oldest granddaughter still a toddler when my son brought him home as a puppy. But Dale was foremost Charlie's dog. My oldest son had always had a special affinity for animals, sometimes more than with people. He'd loved Dale dearly, the dog his most constant confidant and friend. How could Charlie abandon his faithful companion to wonder forever where his beloved master had gone and why he wasn't coming back?

Swirled with the anger was my own confusion and self-doubt. What kind of a woman was I to bear a son who could perpetrate such horrible deeds? What kind of a mother had not noticed the darkness in her own son? What had I missed? What clues had I ignored?

To strive for understanding, I had to go back. Back to the beginning. Not only Charlie's beginning, but my own.

3

Beginnings

Who shall separate us from the love of Christ? Shall trouble or hardship or persecution or famine or nakedness or danger or sword?

—Romans 8:35

I was born with club feet.

This first small storm in my tranquil life-valley left no lingering impact, except that I would pass on those faulty genes to my firstborn son, Charlie. What other faults lying unseen and dormant within him could I attribute to my own genetic makeup?

For my parents, this must have been a frightening and stressful period, since in 1951 corrective measures for such a disability were less developed than Chuck and I would find as parents more than two decades later. But I remember none of this. My memories begin when I was running around healthy and straight-legged in an idyllic setting for childhood, surrounded

by a large extended family of adults and children who filled
my life with laughter, fun, and love. Even looking back over
the decades, I can see no storm clouds, hardly even the slightest
drizzle to mar those childhood memories.

My birth certificate says that I was born in Columbia, Pennsylvania. But I was still a toddler in 1953 when we moved to
nearby Holtwood, so it is that beautiful region that colors my
memories. Holtwood is a small town near the banks of the
Susquehanna River in southern Lancaster County. Its greatest claim to fame is the Holtwood Dam, oldest of three dams
spanning that section of the Susquehanna River, built and maintained by the Holtwood Hydroelectric Plant, one of the area's
main employers. None of which mattered to me as a child,
except that the building of Holtwood Dam had also created
Lake Aldred. This man-made reservoir was popular for fishing,
boating, water-skiing, even white-water rafting where runoff
spilling over the dam created turbulent currents.

One reason for our move to Holtwood was that my paternal
grandparents lived there. My mother came from a large Swiss-
Irish family, the youngest of six siblings. The Haldemans were
a jolly, boisterous clan, always enjoying a good party. My ma-
ternal grandfather owned a grocery store in Columbia (where
I was born) on the corner of Sixth and Walnut Streets. It was a
bustling place, and when we'd travel back to Columbia, I loved
to go visit Pappy, as I called him. When he had a free moment,
Pappy would tell stories about his heritage and living through
World War II, or sing in his powerful, rollicking voice. He was
a member of a barbershop quartet and sang as well with the
Knights of Columbus.

In contrast, my father's heritage was German, and I remember my Neustadter relations as much more structured and focused on work, although they loved fun as well. My paternal

grandparents had a farm with lots of fruit trees, cows, pigs—a wonderland for a small girl. My parents were given a piece of that land and built a home over the hill from them next to the woods. Building a home next to family was a tradition we would eventually carry on, Charlie and Marie in their turn.

For me it was the best of both worlds. From our home, I hiked up into the woods, exploring and dreaming up my own make-believe adventures. And I loved visiting my dad's parents on the farm, picking cherries, helping feed the animals. One of Grandma Neustadter's pastimes was making artificial flowers. Making them together became a special bond between us. Grandma Neustadter would pour molten plastic into the molds. I would carefully place the wires that would become branches and stems. Then we'd bake the molds in the oven. Out would come beautiful flower arrangements.

Once every year, when Philadelphia hosted its annual flower show, Grandma Neustadter would take me out of school. Together we explored the flower show, marveling at the variety and colors. Before heading home, we'd stop at a glassblower's booth, and Grandma would let me choose one of the delicately handcrafted creations to add to my collection.

About the time we moved to Holtwood, my younger brother, Joe, was born, then my younger sister, Jean, five years later. With them and countless cousins and neighborhood friends, I played softball in the meadow, swam in the creek, or hiked up to a nearby Christian retreat, Camp Andrews, whose staff permitted us to swim in the pool when campers were not in residence. Every Easter weekend, when spring had begun restoring green to the woods, we'd gather with neighborhood friends for what we called our Easter picnic. Traveling through the woods, we'd pick out a nice, flat rock to sit on and share all the goodies we'd brought along.

In all these years, I was aware that we shared the beautiful countryside with another significant people group—the Amish. Their horse-drawn buggies, seventeenth-century clothing, and neat farms were part of the landscape, not to mention a major tourist attraction that drew thousands of visitors to congest our country roads every summer. But growing up my only personal contact with this subculture was responding to the occasional wave from an Amish child as our car passed a buggy or scooter.

If our own country lifestyle held more modern conveniences than that of the Amish, it was not without challenges. My father worked at the time—in fact for his entire career—for Armstrong World Industries, an international corporation that specialized in floors, ceilings, and other products related to housing construction. Armstrong was—and is—based out of Lancaster and one of the county's largest employers. My father drove each day into Lancaster for work. In the winter, snow and icy roads often stranded him there.

I remember especially a big snowstorm in 1957. So much snow fell that the drifts were higher than my head. Though the hydroelectric plant was only a few miles away, its services had been disrupted by the storm, leaving the area without light or heat. My mother dug through the snowbanks to the neighbors so that we could walk over and share the warmth of their gas stove. I can still remember my uncle skiing down the hill to bring us milk, since the roads were impassable. Dad didn't make it home that time for an entire week.

And even in my own happy haze of childhood, I recognized vaguely that life was not always so idyllic for others. I had one uncle who suffered from mental illness. He had six children, and I remember one of his daughters near my own age inviting me home with her during my early elementary years. As we approached the house, we heard horrendous screaming and yelling.

"Oh, that's my sister practicing for her play," my cousin quickly informed me. Then as the screaming grew louder and more obvious, she admitted, "No, that's my dad."

I was far from always being an angel. When I was in second grade, I recall being jealous of two of the more popular girls in school. They both wore glasses, so I decided I needed a pair. I convinced my mother I couldn't see to read the blackboard at school. My mother took me to several optometrists. Their diagnosis was that my eyes were fine. But I insisted, and my mother finally found an optometrist who agreed that I needed glasses.

It was a huge lie, of course. Guilt began eating away at me, especially when I saw how worried my mother was. Even at that young age, I recognized that it was a great financial hardship for my parents to purchase the eyeglasses. Finally one day I could keep it in no longer. My mother was down in the basement doing laundry. Sitting on the top basement step, I began to cry.

"Mommy, I have something I have to tell you!" I sobbed.

She came up to put her arm around me, and with tears I confessed how I'd lied. I just wanted to wear glasses. I didn't need them. She forgave me, but I was very remorseful and vowed never to lie again.

It was not just to my mother I made that pledge, but to God. My love for God at this time and my faith in God's love for me were as trusting and unquestioning as my love for my family and the certainty of their love for me. My mother's family was Catholic, an integral part of their Irish heritage. My father came from a Mennonite background, but he was not particularly religious and willingly converted to Catholicism so they could raise their children in the church. I enjoyed going to church on Sundays, vacation Bible school in the summers, and being involved in myriad church activities.

For three weeks each summer, I stayed with my Haldeman grandparents, sleeping on a sofa in the living room. Pappy suffered from muscular dystrophy and by this time was unable to climb stairs, so his bed was placed in the living room for easier care and to allow him to participate in the family's daily routine. At night, tucked into my makeshift bed on the sofa, I would listen to him pray aloud the litany of traditional prayers that were his bedtime routine, including the Lord's Prayer and others I'd memorized in church. Listening to his soft whispers to God, I'd drift off to sleep feeling wrapped securely within the love of God and family.

Of course, if my faith was trusting and unquestioning, it was also unchallenged. I believed because I chose to believe. But also because I'd never been given reason to doubt a loving heavenly Father and Creator of all.

4

Lancaster

Trust in the LORD with all your heart and lean not on your
own understanding; in all your ways submit to him, and
he will make your paths straight.

—Proverbs 3:5–6

By 1963 my father had grown tired of snowy weather, icy roads,
and the long commute in general. So we moved into Lancaster
City, where we were just a short drive from his job at Armstrong
Linoleum. Our home on East Ross Street was in the heart of
old Lancaster, not more than a mile or so from the town center.
The streets were made up of quaint European-style row houses
with steep, pointed gables and a roofed front porch where residents would gather in the evenings to enjoy a cooling breeze
and visit with their neighbors.

I wasn't completely upset about moving. By that time I was
in sixth grade at the public elementary school I attended in

Holtwood, and I was dealing with some turmoil in my life—a boy who constantly picked on me. These days, a bully might get immediate attention from the school administration. In those days, tattling to adults was frowned upon; one simply did their best to survive. But I remember one occasion when a fall off my bike left me with a head injury that required stitches. The thick bandaging gave my head the appearance of being topped with a white box, and for some reason, incomprehensible to me, this boy found my headgear hilarious.

Perhaps he only meant to test the cushioning limitations of the bandage when he struck me with a baseball bat right on my stitches. But I was left furious and afraid. I didn't know how to handle the situation. Moving seemed like a good option. In my mind, I'd convinced myself city kids would be better behaved than country kids. Especially when I found out I'd no longer be attending public school, but a Catholic parochial school where students attended Mass every day. Surely in such an environment, the children would sport halos on their heads!

Transitioning from country living to the city proved to be a major culture shock, but I soon found myself enjoying my new setting. Saint Anne's Parochial School was close enough to walk to instead of taking a bus. I made new friends. But I soon found out human nature was no different in the city—or in a Christian school.

The class to which I was assigned had two boys who were just as naughty as the nemesis I'd left behind in Holtwood. I'd become friends with another girl in the class who was always well-behaved and, for that reason, a favorite of the nun who taught our class. Whether due to our friendship or because I too did my best to study hard and behave properly, the nun chose the two of us for an assignment. We were each given a ruler and seated behind the two misbehaving boys. It was our responsibility to snap our assigned delinquent with the ruler every time he misbehaved. (I don't need to be told that giving a child such an assignment today would be far from politically correct!)

I did my job faithfully for about two weeks before it sunk in that being the class disciplinarian was hardly improving my popularity among my new classmates. Going to the teacher, I begged to be let out of the assignment. She agreed, and thus ended my only stint in law enforcement.

The greatest upheaval that first year in Lancaster was the assassination of President John F. Kennedy on Friday, November 22, at 12:30 p.m. I've often heard people say they remember exactly where they were when they heard the news. I was sitting in class at Saint Anne's, and I remember well the shock and horror that swept the room as the teacher made the announcement.

Now I have people tell me they remember exactly what they were doing when they heard about the Nickel Mines Amish school tragedy. The only silver lining is that everyone I've heard make such a statement has gone on to say that they immediately started praying for all the families involved—including my own.

Within my small universe of Lancaster County, life and school followed a smooth, steady course throughout my teen years. I can give credit for this, above all, to my parents. My siblings and I were so blessed to come from a family that modeled Christlike love. I cannot remember ever witnessing any serious tension between my parents. There was a mutual attitude of submissiveness through surrender, each wanting to serve the other. Mom was the mother to whom all my friends came with those teen questions they were afraid to ask their own parents. My father was dedicated to his family, always interacting with us and carving out time to participate in our activities. We were a normal, flawed family, but his deep, unconditional love made it easy for me to comprehend the love of a perfect heavenly Father.

The only time I remember my father's wrath was when I was thirteen years old. I'd sassed my mother and then locked myself in my room. Talking back to my mother was a show of disrespect my father would not tolerate. When I wouldn't open my door, he promptly broke it down. My young lady status at thirteen was not enough to save me from a spanking. I never talked back to my mother again.

Overall, I worked hard to be a good student and an obedient daughter. If my faith in God was not always a conscious part of my thoughts and activities, it was an underlying foundation I took for granted. I loved daily Mass. I joined the choir and loved singing my heart out for Jesus, the Son of God who died on the cross to pay the penalty for my sins. The image at the front of the sanctuary of that broken body stretched upon a cross and crowned with thorns was an ever-present reminder of His sacrifice for me.

My greatest spiritual dilemma in those years was my fear that God would call me to be a nun. By my teen years I had admittedly more frivolous interests. When I was in eighth grade, the Beatles became the big rage. My friends and I collected trading cards with their pictures. My favorite was Ringo Starr, oddly enough, because he was the least good-looking of all of them—and therefore seemed to me more real. I'd decided that if I ever got a chance to marry one of them, it would be Ringo.

That chance, alas, never came. But by high school, clothing fashion had become a new passion of mine, and I dreamed of becoming a model or an airline stewardess. By then I'd reached my full height, and at just under five foot, eight inches, my tall, slender frame fit the part. My mother encouraged my dreams, even making arrangements for me to attend a local finishing school called Miss Elene's. My younger brother and sister ridiculed me as I practiced floating down steps with a book on my head. I ignored them, and by the time finishing school graduation came, complete with debutante gown and gloves, my self-image was of a sophisticated, cultured young woman.

Certain young men seemed to find me attractive, and there was no denying I enjoyed their company in return. My interest in fashion grew. I loved searching out the newest styles. I must have had one of the first maxi coats in Lancaster County. The last thing I wanted was to spend my life wearing an unfashionable habit and wimple, locked away with solely female companionship in a convent somewhere. So I prayed fervently throughout high school that God would not call me to be a nun.

But by the end of my school years, my prayers had dwindled to mere formality. It was not that I believed less in God or doubted in any way His existence or sovereignty. It was just that I had other priorities. Life was good, and life was busy.

While I'd kept my promise to my mother—and God—never to lie openly again, I was not above small rebellions. Miniskirts were the "cool" dress for young women in the sixties. Knowing my mother wouldn't approve, I acquired a few and would leave the house in one outfit, then change into a miniskirt in a nearby gas station restroom before heading out with my friends. I experimented mildly with alcohol.

When I graduated from high school in 1969, I will admit I wasn't a particularly mature or serious-minded young woman. I began working full-time doing secretarial work at Armstrong World Industries. While still in high school I had dated a young man named Rick. He'd joined the air force, so our relationship consisted of long-distance letter writing. I'd enjoyed some local success in modeling. But my long-term goals remained to get out of Lancaster, go somewhere more inspiring, and do something exciting with my life.

In September 1969, those goals turned upside down. I never did leave Lancaster County. I never became a model or an airline stewardess. But I've never regretted the change in my life course, because I have Chuck, our family, and renewed faith.

On the night of the Miss America pageant my friend Barbara called. With my passion for fashion, my plans for the evening were to watch the pageant and take note of the latest styles of ball gowns and swimsuits. Barbara had other ideas—and not just for her own evening. Her date, Fred, had a friend, an "older man" of twenty-one, who had just returned home that very day from serving with the marine corps in Vietnam. Would I be willing to go on a double date with them that evening?

A marine returned from battle offered a romantic image. But I was far more interested in the beauty pageant. Nor was I in any way interested in pursuing a relationship despite the lukewarm nature of my correspondence with Rick. I was, after all, only biding my time to find a way out of small-town life in Lancaster County. But my friend pleaded, and at last I agreed.

When I told my parents of my evening plans, they reminded me of their strict rule. Any guy I wanted to date had to first be vetted and approved by my parents. Barbara talked to Fred, Fred talked to his friend, and the three agreed to stop by our house to meet my parents before we headed out on our double date.

I didn't have to wait long before a dark green Pontiac Firebird pulled up in front of my house. A stranger was at the wheel, Barb and Fred in the backseat. As the driver stepped out, I had my first glimpse of Charles Carl Roberts III—or Chuck, as his friends called him. He was tall, clean-cut, fit and tan from his military service, polite, and well-spoken as he introduced himself to my parents. In other words, he was one handsome specimen of a man.

But at that point I was more impressed with the car than its driver. Chuck had shed his uniform for the T-shirt and cutoffs of civilian youth. But instead of the "in" style with frayed edges, someone—his mother?—had neatly hemmed them. Had marine units engaged in mortal combat in the jungles of Vietnam missed the memo on proper casual fashion mores? Not cool!

And so we went out for the evening, but it was so unmemorable, I can't remember where. I only recall arriving home unhappy that the Miss America pageant was over and I'd missed the crowning! As to my date, my verdict was that Fred's friend seemed decent enough, but just a bit stuffy with his crew cut and hemmed shorts for my freewheeling tastes. Though that dark green Firebird wasn't half bad!

The very next evening, Barbara and I headed to McDonald's, at the time Lancaster's most popular teen hangout. As we entered, I immediately spotted Chuck's tall, muscular frame among the throng. He was talking to another girl—very pretty— his lean, handsome features lit up with a smile as they chatted easily. Something stirred inside me. Jealousy? Which was crazy since I didn't really even like the guy!

Chuck couldn't have been too taken with the girl, though, because he soon drifted over to talk to me. By the end of the evening, he'd asked me for another date. Solo. I enjoyed spending time getting to know Chuck one-on-one. He was quiet, more prone to listen than to talk, but what he had to say was thoughtful and intelligent. This time I came home considerably more impressed. I guess he was too, because within a week we were dating frequently.

But I still maintained correspondence with Rick. He was stationed at an air force base in England, but due for discharge soon. I'd agreed to see him when he arrived home, though I let him know I was regularly dating another guy. In November, Rick called to let me know his arrival date. We made plans to spend the day visiting Rick's relatives. I informed Chuck. Chuck was not happy about my spending a day with another man, but I explained that Rick and his relatives were longtime family friends. Bottom line, I'd made a commitment to Rick, and I was going to keep it.

Chuck made no further protest, but he asked me to call him when I got home. Rick picked me up, and we had a wonderful day together visiting his various family members. It was close to 11 p.m. by the time we arrived back at my house. I invited Rick inside but reminded him I'd promised to call Chuck first thing. Chuck must have been sitting at the phone, waiting for my call (there were no cell phones or even mobile phones at the time!), because he picked up halfway through the first ring.

"I'm home," I informed him. "And Rick is here."

"I'll be right over," Chuck answered.

The dial tone indicated he'd already hung up. Though Chuck lived some distance away, he was knocking at the front door within twenty minutes. I introduced him to Rick, and the two men shook hands. Then Rick began to talk. Unlike Chuck, he was an eloquent talker. For the next twenty minutes he laid out for Chuck all the reasons why I needed to experience the world and life before settling down with one person.

Chuck made little response, but his eyes never left my face as Rick talked. I just kept looking from Rick to Chuck. Though I didn't know it at the time, my parents were upstairs, their bedroom door open, listening to the discussion.

When Rick finally wound down, Chuck turned to me, his tone quiet but firm. "I have only one thing to say, Terri. I love you. But I will not share you with anyone."

Looking at Rick, I said, "I think that's your cue."

44

Rick's expression was not happy, but he shrugged. "Okay, if that's how you feel." He turned to Chuck, and the two shook hands again.

"Maybe we can get together for a beer sometime," Rick said lightly. Then he walked out the door. I never saw Rick again.

I found out later that after Chuck left, my mom told my dad, "That's the man Terri's going to marry."

If our relationship had a single drawback, it was that Chuck had no interest in attending church with me nor spoke at all about spiritual issues. His upbringing did not include church attendance, though he remembered making a profession of faith in Christ as a child attending vacation Bible school. I didn't count his current lack of faith as a major stumbling block. After all, my father had not been particularly religious when he married my mother. But he'd joined the Catholic Church to please her when the children came along, and I'd been witness to his quiet faith over the years. Besides, my own faith walk was far from a priority in my life at this time. What mattered was that Chuck was a wonderful young man, and I was falling more deeply in love every day.

By Christmas, Chuck had asked me to marry him. We began planning a May wedding but soon decided we couldn't wait that long. So on March 14, 1970, I walked down my last runway—not a fashion runway, but the center aisle of Saint Anne's Catholic Church. Floating down the aisle on my father's arm, I felt like a princess, my bridal gown a vision of white lace, frothy mantilla veil, and long gloves. My prince in his tuxedo stood tall and handsome at the altar. My joy overflowed as we exchanged vows and I became his wife. I was just eighteen, Chuck twenty-one.

My Uncle Jake—a professional singer—provided the music for our reception at the Circle M Ranch, a famed local Western-themed resort. The song he crooned as we stepped out onto the polished floor of the reception hall for our first dance as a married couple was a lover's song. And as I whirled my full lace skirts, clasped tightly in my new husband's loving embrace, I harbored no doubts that my life from that point on would embody a fairy tale's "happily ever after."

5

Invasion

I remember my affliction and my wandering, the bitterness and the gall. . . . Yet this I call to mind and therefore I have hope: Because of the LORD's great love we are not consumed, for his compassions never fail. They are new every morning; great is your faithfulness.

—Lamentations 3:19–23

The doorbell ended any further introspection. My friend Delores, with whom I'd eaten lunch—was it really only a few hours ago?—and her husband, Mike, both of them co-workers at Sight & Sound Theatre, were the first to arrive, then some of our closest friends from church. With each new arrival there were hugs, prayers, tears. And with each we tried to offer some kind of explanation.

I longed for quiet and solitude to process my own thoughts and grief. But I also craved the distraction of people swirling around me, the bustle of serving hot drinks, accepting gifts of food, greeting one visitor after another, all the welcome commotion with which our culture tries to alleviate the pain of sudden loss. Mike, Delores, Joe, Barb, Nate, Jean, Randy, Melissa, Serena, Eric, Tyler, Pastor Dwight, Dan, Pastor Stewart, Betsy, Henry, and many more—thank you all for being God's angels of grace and healing to us that day.

Far less welcome were media personnel now swarming the perimeter of our front yard. Vans with the call letters of local and national TV and radio stations lined the shoulder of the road. News crews hoisted huge cameras and thrust microphones at visitors as they stepped out of their cars. We'd made it clear that reporters were not welcome at our door or trespassing on our lawn. But as visitors found parking along the street and walked up to our house, the newspeople called out questions and waylaid anyone willing to stop.

Why can't they leave us alone? I wailed mentally. They were only doing their jobs, I knew. But the invasion of our private mourning and worry about how they might be portraying our son and our family hammered at my head and heart until I felt sick.

I considered going out to make a brief statement. Maybe I could give another side to the story. What could I have said in the face of the day's events? But Chuck, well-experienced in dealing with the media, and always my protector, immediately stepped in to prevent me.

Soon my parents drove up, and the news crews rushed toward them. My mother, always outgoing and friendly, paused as a question was shouted out. Someone thrust a microphone to catch her answer. Instantly one of our visiting friends placed himself between the reporter and my mother, shepherding her and my father inside the house.

My mother was grateful for the intervention. I don't know what she saw in my expression as she hugged me. But I will never forget the anguish in her eyes as she looked at my dear friend Delores: "Delores, I have always been there for my daughter. But I can't now. I am too weak. Can you be there for her? She is so fragile." I felt as vulnerable as a crystal vase slamming into concrete.

Chuck had already called our youngest son, Jon, and his wife, Megan, who had been married just a year, to let them know what had happened. Jon had always looked up to his big brother and was, of course, devastated.

By now Chuck had also managed to contact our second son, Josh, who was in Louisiana on a reconstruction project. But I was the one who called Zach, our third son, who was living in Manhattan. He'd been away from home for several years by this time, first in Florida, where he'd attended film school, and then New York. While our other sons joined us for every holiday and many family activities, Zach had been unable to travel home often in recent years.

Our sons were not close in age. Josh was born three years after Charlie, Zach five years, and Jon was almost a decade younger. But once they reached adulthood, they seemed to enjoy each other's company when they were together. So I was stunned when Zach replied angrily to the news. He knew more of the day's horror than I did, the details having already been broadcast all over New York.

When I told him I'd let him know the service arrangements as soon as I knew them, he responded vehemently: "I will not be coming to my brother's funeral. I hate him for what he's done—to those girls, to our family. I will not honor him by being present!"

I cried and pleaded, but it only intensified Zach's resolve. Before the call ended it was obvious that no amount of begging from his mother was going to change his heart and mind.

I was heartbroken. Chuck and I needed our sons with us to face the next days and, above all, Charlie's funeral. Marie's children adored their Uncle Zach. They needed his presence too. But Zach had made it clear he would not be moved. How could I ask him to forgive his brother when I was struggling with how I could forgive Charlie myself?

There was one thing I could do. Though I could barely choke out a prayer myself, I began asking everyone who walked through the door to pray for Zach. Especially that he would change his mind and come home in time for his brother's funeral.

Through all this, Chuck had been a pillar of strength to me, doing whatever needed to be done, dealing with law enforcement, visitors, and the media. But when there were no new crises to tackle, he slumped down at the breakfast bar, his head low, tears streaming unchecked down his face. I knew the shame and guilt that were overwhelming him because I felt it too. Our son had done this thing. Though we were not the perpetrators, we had given birth to him, had raised him. All the reputation for integrity, honorable living, and Christian charity for which the Roberts name had been synonymous in this community had been swept away.

Beyond the influx of visitors, our phone had not stopped ringing all day. Among the callers were police officers with whom my husband had worked for so many years. They were calling to express support and encouragement, but my husband could not even take their calls. The shame and embarrassment were too great. His palpable grief and pain were as inconsolable as the biblical King David's mourning of the death of his own traitorous son, Absalom, and I knew my husband's heart held the same agonized cry: "O my son [Charlie]! My son, my son [Charlie]! If only I had died instead of you—O [Charlie], my son, my son!" (See 2 Samuel 18:33.)

My heart broke for my husband, but there was nothing I could do to ease his pain. Then, as though God himself were reaching down from heaven with a comforting touch, I watched a miracle unfold. Through the window I caught sight of a stalwart figure dressed in black. It was our neighbor Henry Stoltzfoos, whose father, Jake, had sold my parents the land on which our house stood. He was dressed in his formal visiting attire and wide-brimmed straw hat.

Striding up to the front door, Henry knocked. Outside, the newspeople had already jerked to full alert, curious as to why an Amishman would be knocking on a Roberts' door on this day of all days. Surely there must be a story here!

I wondered too. Henry was part of the Amish community. He had friends, even relatives, whose daughters had died in that schoolhouse. Like all the Amish, he had every reason to hate us right now. All the years of peaceful coexistence as neighbors, working together with my husband to provide transportation for the Amish, would count for nothing now.

But Henry didn't look angry as we welcomed him into the house. Instead, compassion radiated from his face. Walking straight over to Chuck, who still sat slumped at the breakfast bar, he put one hand on his shoulder. The first words I heard him speak took my breath away: "Roberts, we love you. This was not your doing. You must not blame yourself."

Henry: The Beginning of Forgiveness

I'd known the Roberts family for a long time. Back in the early seventies, when Terri's parents bought the lot next to our house from my father, Terri's younger sister Jean and I used to ride our horses together. Their horse barn was my first construction assignment. Later, when Terri and her family built their house on the neighboring spot, I saw her boys grow up, playing in the yard. Sometimes we would come over to swim in their pool. In the spring of 2006, Roberts—that's what I call Terri's husband—started doing taxi work for me. He was the driver for our youth singing activities. We became friends during our many drives, sharing a bit of our personal lives. I remember him telling me he had a son who drove a milk truck.

On October 2, 2006, I was at my shop building furniture when I heard the news about the shooting. A little later, my son Aaron came home and told me that the gunman was Terri and Roberts' oldest son. My first reaction was that they must have gotten the names mixed up. This just couldn't be right! When I saw the media trucks starting to flock outside their house, I realized that it must be true.

I'm a board member of the three Amish schools in the area. We decided as a board to have a talk with our teachers that same afternoon to calm them down and show our support. Before we went over there, I thought I should go down to see Terri and Roberts. But when I saw how many media trucks were outside, I thought maybe this wasn't such a good time. We met with the teachers. When the driver let me off at my house, I again started across the road to the Roberts' house. But I felt very weak, like I wasn't going to be able to go through with it. Changing my mind, I headed toward my own driveway instead.

I started up the quarter-mile driveway and the good Lord was telling me, "You need to go talk to Roberts." So I turned around. I felt weak and turned away from Roberts' house. When I turned away I would get weaker yet. I went toward Roberts' house. That gave me more strength. When I turned toward Roberts' I felt weak, but not as weak as when retreating back up my long lane.

At last I stood at their door and knocked. I almost walked away again. *What am I doing here?* I thought to myself. Then I saw somebody peek through the window.

"It's an Amishman!" the person exclaimed. A man responded, "Let him in."

When the door opened, I saw a good number of people inside—friends and family members—and various conversations going on everywhere. But it was Roberts himself who caught my immediate attention. I had never heard a man cry so loud. He was completely bent over, his head on the counter, a cloth in his hand soaked with tears. I have boys myself, and I tried to imagine how I would feel if it had been one of my boys. Walking up to him, I started to gently stroke his shoulders, not saying anything. I did it to comfort him, but I also needed something to hold on to because my legs were shaking and my heart was beating so hard. I stood there for a good five minutes, neither of us saying a word.

Then suddenly Roberts began to speak. It was not a cry of self-pity. He was crying for everyone but himself: "All those poor mothers. All those poor grandmothers. Those poor, poor parents. All those poor children. Those poor teachers." He continued repeating over and over every possible victim of the tragedy. "And my baby boy I loved so much. If he would have just shared with me how bad he felt. My baby boy. I just wish I could have been a better father. We can't stay here. The only thing left to do now is to move as far away from the Amish as we can."

He finally broke off. But after a moment of silence, he started the circle again, repeating what he had just said. Then again, and again. After a good half hour, I found the strength to interrupt him. "Roberts, I think the devil used your boy. It wasn't your boy. It was the devil who used your boy."

For the first time that evening, Roberts lifted his head from the counter to look at me. "Do you really think that's what it was?"

"Yes," I said. "I think the devil used your boy."

"Thank you, Henry," he answered. It was like a sparkle of hope was ignited in his eyes.

Up until this point I had felt completely helpless. Now my strength came back to me. It was the Lord God who brought hope to Roberts, not me. The good Lord sent me there and was talking through me. I think this was the beginning of forgiveness.

———◆———

For more than an hour, Henry stood by my husband, consoling him and affirming his love and forgiveness. Above all, Henry kept reassuring Chuck that there was no reason for us to move. The Amish did not hold Chuck or any of the Roberts family responsible for Charlie's actions. By the time he left, my husband was sitting up straight, some of the burden clearly eased from his shoulders. For Chuck, it was not only the beginning of forgiveness, but also of healing.

To this day I call Henry "my angel in black." His act of grace and forgiveness in the face of the terrible loss he and his community had just endured had an impact that cannot be measured. Not just on our family, but on so many others who came to hear the story, including the media, who seized on this story as far more interesting—and puzzling—than the original tragedy itself. Nor was Henry's gesture unique. Over the next weeks, we would encounter repeatedly gifts of love, forgiveness, and acceptance from the Amish community.

And above all, at Charlie's funeral. But I will tell that story later.

For my part, I was still battling the devastation of Zach's refusal to come to the funeral. My family was crumbling around me. The world in which I stood kept shifting from reality to non-reality and back again. This could not be happening. And yet it was. This was surely not real, but a nightmare from which I would awake. But no, it was real. I was awake.

A special comfort came when my nephew Travis stopped by. "Aunt Terri, you were a good mom," he kept assuring me. "You are a good mom."

"What kind of mother could I have been?" I asked painfully. "How can this be? What did I miss that this could have happened?"

"Don't say that!" he responded. "You were a good mom. Such a good mom, I often wished you were my mom."

Another nephew, Nate, reiterated the same sentiments. He asked if he could sing to me, then sang a wonderfully comforting inspirational song he'd composed.

And then my friend Betsy offered me comfort that has remained with me. My own personal "day one" hero, Betsy is a counselor from the church my brother attends, Calvary Monument Bible Church. During her visit that first evening, we stood together in the family room.

"How old was your son?" she asked.

"He would have been thirty-three in two months," I told her.

"And from everything I've heard, he was a wonderful son to you."

"Yes, he was an absolutely wonderful son," I responded. I did not want to minimize the evil that Charlie had done. But the truth was that every person who'd shared their memories of Charlie that day had reiterated the son we knew—a quiet, soft-spoken man, but a man who was kind, honest, hardworking, and loving. Certainly no one inside or outside his family had ever glimpsed any reason to be afraid of him. The mental anguish and turmoil he'd expressed in his suicide notes, the reasons he'd given for harboring anger and bitterness against God—did that completely obliterate all we'd seen and known of Charlie for the past thirty-two years?

As though she'd read my mind, Betsy went on: "What happened today was a tiny slice of your son's entire life. When your mind goes there, don't stop. Let it go back further to the thirty-two years of wonderful memories you have. Refocus on those memories, not the events of this day."

Her advice was such a consolation to me as well as a great support in the days ahead, even to the present. My mind does not go to the events at the school as often now, but when it does, I don't try to stop it. I can never ignore what happened. The devastation of that day will never go away, and its effects of loss, pain, and sorrow are still being felt by the families involved. But when I do remember that day and still shed tears over those memories, it has been greatly helpful and healing to follow Betsy's recommendation and take my thoughts further back, to flood my mind with wonderful memories of the times we had as a family. Charlie was not perfect, and the choices he made in the last hours of his life were dark and twisted beyond my understanding. But for more than three decades he'd been a loving and loved son. And that was the gift Betsy gave back to me that night.

As Betsy left that evening, I allowed my mind to drift back again over the years. This time not to my own beginnings, but to Charlie's.

6

Charlie

Ask and it will be given to you; seek and you will find.
—Matthew 7:7

Only one thing remained to complete my fairy tale.

Marriage to Chuck proved exciting for a girl still in her teens. We moved into an apartment my parents owned right across East Ross Street from them. Chuck soon moved on from working as a mason to a good position at Armstrong Ceiling Plant. But his ambition was to become a police officer. His military training and strong, competent personality made law enforcement a perfect fit. Chuck entered the ten-week police training program, and in 1972 he joined Manor Township Police Department. He would go on to earn a degree in law enforcement from Penn State and serve more than thirty years with MTPD, eventually rising to sergeant.

My parents loved Chuck, but his penchant for fast, sporty means of transportation raised my mother's eyebrows. The dark green Firebird was followed by seven other cars and a motorcycle within our first two years of marriage. My mother, with her wry Irish humor, commented, "I'm sure glad he doesn't trade in his women like he does his cars!"

So was I. (Four and a half decades later, we are still married, and our love has grown far stronger and sent down deep roots since the young passion of our early years.) But by this time in my story, Chuck was a policeman, and I was aware that people in his profession ranked among the highest in divorce rates. As a young policeman's wife, I was invited to classes to help me understand the stresses he faced. A majority of his law enforcement colleagues were divorced. Attending those classes gave me a determination that Chuck and I were going to work on our marriage to keep it healthy.

I continued working at Armstrong World Industries. But I longed to be a mother as well as a wife. A year or so after our wedding, I suffered a miscarriage. Neither Chuck nor I was attending church at this time. We were both working full-time, and weekends when Chuck wasn't on patrol were our time to be together as a couple. Though I'd pushed my faith to a back burner, I remember well praying fervently that God would allow me to get pregnant.

God answered my prayers. On December 7, 1973, almost four years after our wedding, our firstborn son, Charles Carl Roberts IV, was laid in my arms at Lancaster General Hospital. But my joy turned to tears as the doctor began explaining that there was a problem. My precious baby boy was not perfect—not even normal. I could see at a glance that his tiny feet were twisted into the same ugly club position that my own had been.

This was no gentle cloudburst, but a life storm. Worse, it was my child who bore the brunt of it. And I discovered—as mothers have through the generations—how much more my child's suffering could tear at my heart than any storms I had borne myself. I was not only distraught, but I couldn't help feeling a certain responsibility. Why shouldn't my husband blame me for his firstborn's abnormality? It was from my faulty genes that my baby had inherited this deformity.

But Chuck never made me feel at fault. From the moment he took his son into his arms, he loved Charlie unconditionally. We both did. And the pediatrician was optimistic. The recommended treatment of casts and braces, probably even surgery when Charlie was older, to force my son's twisted feet into proper position, would not be pleasant. But with time, there was every hope he would eventually walk and grow normally.

If I did not remember my own discomfort as an infant, I felt every moment of Charlie's. The casts were heavy and cumbersome, and since their purpose was to force his tiny feet out of their unnatural alignment, they were also painful. Charlie's screams tore at my heart. The worst was when his casts had to be changed, which was every couple of weeks due to his rapid growth. This involved dunking him over and over into a sink of water to soak off the plaster of Paris so that the bandages could be unwound. Then there was the excruciating ordeal of readjusting his diminutive limbs before rewrapping, and holding him still long enough for the plaster of Paris to harden in its new position.

Thankfully, by the end of six months the casts were discontinued. For the next two years, Charlie wore braces, but eventually this too was reduced to the nighttime hours. As expected, Charlie's walking skills developed later than normal. But by the time he turned three, he was running around. As with my own childhood experience, he seemed to have no memory of the pain or constraints. In fact, Charlie healed so well that when I took him back for a follow-up consultation at six years old, the specialist decided he wouldn't need surgery after all.

I could not easily forget my faith. Before Charlie's birth, I began attending church again. My continuing to do so was not because of a renewed prayer life or closeness to God. Simply put, I was a mother, and I wanted my children to enjoy the same rich heritage of faith and church I had experienced growing up. While faith was not at this time a central part of Chuck's world, he honored me by at least attending Christmas and Easter church celebrations with me.

Over the next years, our family expanded. Our second son, Joshua, was born one day before Charlie's third birthday. Zachary arrived twenty-two months later, and he was almost five when Jonathan was born. I loved my four precious sons, though I sometimes wondered what it would be like to have a daughter, to be laundering frilly little dresses instead of T-shirts and jeans, or fussing with French braids and hair ribbons. I'd have to wait for granddaughters to find out.

By this time we'd moved twice. When my parents relocated to a home in the country just south of Strasburg, we purchased their home on East Ross Street. The row house gave us more room than the apartment where we'd been living, but it had only a tiny backyard and no driveway, so Chuck often had to find parking several blocks away. When Charlie was six years old, we moved again to a suburban neighborhood on the west side of Lancaster City. What a thrill to pull into our own driveway instead of parking down the street!

A new and bigger house was not the only change in my life. Sometime around the birth of my third son, Zach—as he came to be known—my mother started to attend a Bible study.

Though all my family was devout Catholic, in-depth study of Scripture was not part of our heritage. A family Bible had always sat on our coffee table but was only opened to look at the pictures. And though I'd purchased a Bible while in high school, I'd rarely opened it.

Now as my mother began studying the Bible, I saw her change. Her spiritual growth, her deepened faith in God, impressed me. I longed for such a change in my own life. The program my mother attended was called Neighborhood Bible Studies (NBS). When I heard of an organizational meeting being held to start an NBS program for women in our area, I decided to attend. I drove out to the chicken farm where the meeting was held. With a group of other women, I listened to one of the authors of the NBS material share how to knock on doors and invite women to Bible study. You didn't have to be a trained Bible teacher. Each of the women in the group would take turns leading the study from material provided to us.

I'd never taken part in a Bible study, much less led one. Nor did I consider myself in any way a leader. But I could knock on a door. Rather to my own astonishment, I found myself volunteering to start a group. I went door to door throughout my neighborhood.

"I'm starting a group to study the Bible on Wednesday mornings at 9 a.m.," I explained. "It isn't tied to any particular church, just a study to see for ourselves what the Bible has to say."

I wondered if I'd find a single neighbor interested in coming. So I was amazed when a dozen women from my own age to white-haired grandmothers responded. The group represented various church denominations and faith backgrounds. Like me, many were mothers of young children, so we found someone willing to watch the children at one home while we held the

Bible study at another. Each week we would rotate to a different home for child care and study.

Our first Bible study was on the life of Christ as portrayed in the gospel of Mark. I knew Jesus was God's Son. Because I'd always attended church and believed the Bible to be true, I'd never really considered my own need for a Savior. But by the time I'd finished studying the book of Mark, I got down on my knees and surrendered my life in a new way to God, asking forgiveness for my sins and committing my life to Jesus Christ, not just as my Savior, but as Lord of my life in every aspect and every moment.

At this time, Chuck still did not share my interest in spiritual things. His job as a patrol officer kept him busy and away from home for long hours every week. What were his thoughts about my new interest in attending church and studying the Bible? While he said little, he must have approved of the changes he saw in my life and character, because when I asked Chuck if he'd be willing to attend an evening couples' Bible study, he agreed. That was the beginning of Chuck's own journey of faith. Within a short time, he was not only participating in the Bible study, but attending church with the rest of the family.

My hunger to know God more and to understand God's Word continued to grow. I loved being with these other women who were my neighbors, sharing day-to-day issues on husbands, raising children, and family life; praying together; and digging into God's Word to find answers to our questions. I had never felt so secure in who I was and who God was calling me to be as a wife and mother. I look back on my experience in Neighborhood Bible Study—the friendships developed and my own faith growth through studying God's Word—as one of the richest times in my life.

By now I was pregnant with our fourth child. Life changes when you have children. Their hurts become your own. It was one thing to have been careless and dismissive of my faith— to place God on a back burner if not out of my thoughts completely—when life centered on my own wants and enjoyment, even the delight of being wife to the man I loved. But life was different with children to think about, to protect, and to weep over. When I could not spare them from harm or hurt, not to mention a husband whose profession took him into harm's way on a daily basis, I found myself crying out more and more to the only One in whose almighty hands I could place my loved ones' lives and futures. Prayer and memorizing God's promises given in Scripture became my lifeline.

I clung to one such Scripture passage as I sat in my doctor's office, my hands protectively cradling the child growing in my womb.

"The sonogram has revealed a defect," the doctor told me. "Your baby's kidneys are not functioning properly."

There was nothing to be done except wait and hope—and pray. I cried out a passage of Scripture I'd memorized, Matthew 7:7–11:

> Ask and it will be given to you; seek and you will find. . . . Which of you, if your son asks for bread, will give him a stone? Or if he asks for a fish, will give him a snake? If you, then, though you are evil, know how to give good gifts to your children, how much more will your Father in heaven give good gifts to those who ask him!

Heavenly Father, I wouldn't give my son a snake if he were hungry and asking for fish, I prayed. *I know how much I love my own sons. Whatever they needed, I would never turn away from giving it to them. You love me so much more than I can love them. You say to ask and it will be given to me. I am asking you, please heal my baby!*

The rest of my pregnancy was routine. When Jonathan was born healthy and full-term, the doctor found no signs of a kidney defect. He could not explain it. I in turn had no doubt God had answered my prayers with a miracle of healing.

Years later, in the aftermath of the Nickel Mines schoolhouse tragedy, I would cry out in confusion. How is it that God answers one heart cry, but does not answer another equally sincere and urgent? Why does He permit in the lives of His children rain and drought, blue skies and tsunamis? If answered prayer brings strengthened faith, why does He not always respond to the heart cry of His children? How is it that our heavenly Father does indeed appear at times to give a poisonous reptile instead of succulent fish, a cold, hard stone to fill an empty stomach instead of bread?

I cannot claim to have found any definitive answers. But I have found hope. I believe that the almighty Creator who permits tragedies to enter into my life and into the lives of others is the same loving heavenly Father who healed my precious fourth-born in my womb.

I will cling to that hope and conviction even when I do not understand.

7

Homeschooling

Rejoice always, pray continually, give thanks in all circumstances; for this is God's will for you in Christ Jesus.

—1 Thessalonians 5:16–18

When Charlie started school, academics did not come easy for him. Even as a young child, he loved making things with his hands. Building blocks, then Lincoln Logs, then Legos became his favorite toys. Any time he could go to Pop Pop's house to work with his grandfather on a carpentry project was a treat. Charlie loved animals as well. He, more than any of his brothers, would bond with each new dog that became the family pet.

But Charlie struggled with schoolwork. Today he would be diagnosed as having a serious learning disability. At that time I became accustomed to calls from his teachers at Saint Leo's Catholic School, where he attended kindergarten through second grade, concerned that he was not applying himself or falling behind in his homework.

I was just as frustrated as his teachers were. Charlie was a quiet child, well-behaved, always loving and helpful with his younger brothers. In fact, I can remember only one serious disciplinary episode in his entire childhood. At the time, Charlie was six years old, and his brother Joshua was three. We were returning home from a shopping trip to Two Guys, a local department store, when I heard a buzzing sound from the backseat. Glancing back, I asked what the noise was.

"It's nothing," Charlie replied.

I insisted the boys show me what they were playing with. Reluctantly, the boys each held up a Tommie Toy. These were small figures about an inch and a half tall with little windup knobs. When the knob was wound, the figure's little legs would scoot along, creating the buzzing noise I heard.

"Where did you get them?" I asked.

"From the store," Charlie spoke up quickly.

"Did you pay for them?" I demanded.

The two boys' eyes widened as they stared at me, then slowly shook their heads. Looking at them sternly, I asked, "What do you think we should do? Do Mommy and Daddy pay for the things they buy?"

Both boys nodded "yes." By this time we were turning into our own driveway. After Chuck and I talked it over, we decided to call the store and ask if the security guard could talk to the boys about their offense. The guard agreed. The boys counted out money from their piggy banks to pay for the stolen merchandise, and we returned to the store. After the security guard explained to the boys the consequences of theft, they handed over the money. Their punishment was that they would pay for the items but not be allowed to keep them. We never had an issue with theft again.

When I sat down with the school counselor to discuss Charlie's learning difficulties, she began asking about our home life, and then turned her questions to my husband. Her conclusion was that my husband's profession as a police officer kept him from being involved enough in his son's life, which was causing Charlie to act out by not studying. It was a frustrating experience: I was there to get counsel for our son, and the counselor suggested all he needed was a more interactive father.

It was true my husband was quiet, while I was the extrovert of the family. Chuck's more stoic German heritage and his military training did not encourage the open expression of feelings. As a police officer, he did not consider it appropriate to bring home business or talk about the difficult or dangerous aspects of his profession. But he also loved his family dearly and made every effort to spend time with his wife and sons.

That same year my husband and I were invited to participate in a Christian couples' retreat sponsored by a program called Marriage Encounter. Part of the retreat program was writing letters to each other as a couple. I wrote reams to my husband, pouring out my heart and feelings. Chuck in return wrote sentences to me. By the end of the retreat, I recognized that Chuck and I were very different people. I came away from the weekend with some tears, recognizing that this retreat had not miraculously turned my husband into the more expressive, social-oriented person that was my illusion of what he should be.

But as I prayed and sought God's will in all this, I came to recognize that I could walk away from our marriage because my husband didn't write reams of romantic prose or communicate as much as I might like. Or I could choose to appreciate all the countless good qualities that he did have. I could choose to love my husband just as he was: my protector, my provider, the man who loved me with all his heart. I could accept that life is not always—or ever will be—exactly what we want it to be, but we are still called to move forward, not walk away.

That day I chose to love my husband. Again and again in the years ahead, above all when faced with tragedy, I would learn the importance of making right choices: choosing love instead of resentment, forgiveness instead of hate, surrender instead of bitterness.

And I would witness the awful consequences of making the wrong choices.

By the end of second grade, Charlie's misery and the frustration of his teachers had reached a high enough level that we decided to pull him out and try home education. At the time, homeschooling was a new movement, and I knew little about it. But my younger sister, Jean, and her husband, Randy Hildebrand, were homeschooling their growing family, eventually eight children. Close friends of theirs, Chuck and Cathy Powers, were also homeschooling. My parents volunteered to keep Charlie at their house during the school week, where my mother would teach him. Cathy Powers volunteered to work with him one day a week on some of the more challenging subjects.

Charlie was excited at the prospect. As the oldest grandson, he had a special bond with his grandparents, Pop Pop and Baba, as the grandkids called them. It was Charlie who'd first come up with the nickname for my mother while still in his crib. How we laughed when we discovered that "Baba," as he insisted on calling her, meant "old woman" in Russian or "grandma" in Polish.

Even better, Pop Pop and Baba's house was out in the country with lots of woods and fields to explore and a ridge to climb, unlike our suburban home with no basement and three bedrooms. Charlie homeschooled with his grandmother for third and fourth grade, coming home on weekends. Of course, we also saw him often during the week since my parents lived only a few miles away. With individualized attention and studying at his own pace, he soon caught up and began to enjoy school again.

But it was also at Pop Pop and Baba's that trauma again entered Charlie's life. Charlie had always loved animals, and he developed a special bond with Pop Pop and Baba's Siberian husky, Suzie. Suzie reciprocated that affection, providing Charlie a companion and friend into whose long, furry ear he could pour out his thoughts and feelings during the school week when he was away from his brothers and parents.

But Suzie had a fault—wanderlust. Periodically she would break the chain that tethered her in the yard at night and run off with a pack of dogs, eventually returning home unapologetically pleased with herself. But after one escape, Suzie didn't return home. For several days, the entire family turned out to look for Suzie, up and down the country lanes, into the fields and woods, calling her name. But there was no response—and no Suzie.

Then one night several days after Suzie's disappearance, Charlie woke up. He was certain he'd heard Suzie's distinctive bark somewhere nearby. Running to his grandparents' room, he woke them up. "I hear Suzie. She's out there!"

Pop Pop and Baba listened, but if a dog had been barking, nothing could be heard now. "It was probably some neighbor's dog," Pop Pop said at last. "Or you were dreaming."

"But I know it was Suzie," Charlie insisted. "I recognize her bark!"

"It can't be. We've already looked around here," Pop Pop assured Charlie. "Now go back to bed."

Disconsolately, Charlie returned to his bedroom. He'd been so sure, but maybe he had been mistaken. Or maybe he truly had been dreaming. Charlie never heard the barking again, and Suzie never returned home. But weeks later when the corn crop was being harvested, Suzie's body was found in a nearby field. The broken chain still attached to her collar had tangled around the cornstalks so she couldn't free herself. Eventually she had died of thirst and starvation.

Charlie blamed himself. He'd heard Suzie's plea for help, but he'd done nothing. If only he'd gone out that very night to track the barking. If only he'd tried harder to make Pop Pop look for her. But Charlie said little about the tragedy to us or to his grandparents. Instead he buried his anguish deep inside and went on quietly with his life.

Did he continue brooding over Suzie's death? Did he continue blaming himself? I don't know because he never brought up his loss. Only now, looking back over our son's life, can I see the beginnings of a pattern that buried pain and loss, self-blame and bitterness deep within his heart and mind instead of sharing it with others—and perhaps finding his way to forgiveness and acceptance.

8

A New Home

For this reason, since the day we heard about you, we have
not stopped praying for you.

—Colossians 1:9

After Suzie's death, we did our best to comfort Charlie. But
in the busy ebb and flow of life, we quickly put this sad incident behind us. By now our second son, Josh, was also starting school. Charlie's home education had progressed so well
we decided to homeschool his brothers too. The experience
proved fun and productive, but also sometimes frustrating. I
gleaned advice from my sister, Jean, and the Powerses, but also
researched for myself how to go about this new phenomenon
in our society.

I remember well the very first homeschool fair in our area,
where vendors of homeschooling curriculum and products

showed their wares. Held at a small church in East Petersburg, it showcased at most ten vendors. Within two years, the fair had moved to the sizeable auditorium of nearby Lancaster Bible College and soon outgrew that space as well. Our small group was no longer alone in this new venture.

For fifth and sixth grade, we enrolled Charlie in a nearby Christian school, Living Word Academy. With two solid years of homeschooling behind him, Charlie did well there. But the cost of private education was more than we could afford, especially with four sons. So Charlie joined our other three at home.

This proved a wonderful chapter in our lives. All four of our boys loved homeschooling. Once they were older, we told them that if at any point they preferred to transfer to the public or private high school, we would honor their choice. Charlie chose not to, graduating from high school in the homeschooling program. His brothers in turn each attended a year or more at a local Christian high school or public school.

For Charlie, academics would never come easily. But now that he could work at his own speed without the distraction of a noisy class of other children, he had no difficulty keeping up with math, English, and other studies. Personally, I loved the one-on-one contact with my sons as I tutored them. Charlie's favorite class was math, an area in which I'd needed tutoring myself in high school, and I can remember madly studying his algebra lessons the night before so that I could teach them to him.

Nor did Charlie or his brothers suffer socially. Homeschoolers had become a growing demographic in Lancaster County. By this time our friends Chuck and Cathy Powers, who had so graciously helped us start our homeschooling journey, had moved to France to head up a Christian ministry there. But our four sons, my sister's eight kids, my brother's four, and a number of other homeschooling families formed the basis for the area's first homeschool co-op. One day a week, we got together to share writing, art, and other interactive learning projects. As a group we took field trips to Philadelphia, New York, and Washington, D.C. We visited historical sites like Independence Hall and Ellis Island. The kids toured art museums, explored zoos, and visited with representatives at the state capitol in Harrisburg.

The boys enjoyed all types of sports too, playing baseball, soccer, football, and basketball as well as skateboarding and biking. Our homeschool co-op started an annual track and field day where approximately sixty homeschoolers would get together to compete. Charlie and our other sons also enjoyed learning practical skills and earning badges in the Boy Scouts.

By the time Charlie was twelve, he also held his first job—a paper route—diligently heading out every morning in all kinds of weather without complaint. Always industrious, he sought extra jobs like mowing lawns and shoveling snow in order to earn money for a new bike he wanted.

It was about this time we faced a second pet loss. Our dog Cinnamon, who had been part of the family from Charlie's earliest memories, had to be put down. Charlie went with me to the vet. I still remember his bitter tears as we said good-bye. Dogs would always play a special part in Charlie's life. But Charlie evidenced just as tender a heart for human beings in need. He took part in helping a shut-in, and when anyone on his paper route needed help around the house or yard, Charlie was always willing to volunteer. Another traumatic event in Charlie's life was when a neighbor and newspaper customer committed suicide. Charlie stopped by his home just as his wife had found him. We talked about it, but I am not sure what kind of lasting effect this incident may have had on him.

As our boys grew, it became apparent to Chuck and me that each of our sons was very different in personality. Charlie was our introvert, though he was never a recluse. He was always willing to join in family activities. Though never the talkative one, he had a delightful dry sense of humor, and when he did come out with a comment, it held such sharp observation that we would immediately turn to listen. Then he would give his sweet, impish smile, and we would all laugh.

Charlie continued to prefer hands-on learning to books, always wanting to figure things out for himself, and became a skilled carpenter as he worked alongside his grandfather. Though he joined Boy Scouts, baseball, and soccer, he didn't excel in sports as much as his brothers did. But he loved anything outdoors. He took the hunter's safety course at age twelve and became as avid a hunter as his father.

Our second son, Joshua, was the most academic, always willing to help his brothers with their studies. He was far more extroverted than his older brother, and tender and sensitive with others. He too loved to hunt but was also very athletic.

Our third son, Zach, was the most easygoing, an avid basketball player. He found our quiet, rural world more constricting than the others and from an early age expressed a desire to explore and travel. We were not surprised when he became our only son to travel out of state all the way to Florida to attend film school after high school, then taking a job in Manhattan instead of Lancaster County and traveling overseas to Sweden and other countries.

Our youngest son, Jon, was more of an introvert like Charlie. But he was also fearless and daring in sports. He acquired a dirt bike, practicing ultimate stunts with it that would give gray hair to any mother.

For my part, I loved watching each one of them grow up and mature into adults. These were years filled with rich memories.

Though Chuck was not home daily with the boys as I was, he was always there for his family, a devoted husband and dad. We enjoyed spending time together as a family. We went to church together. We took family vacations, including many camping trips with the boys to the beach and wooded areas.

A favorite family trip was to a hunting camp in Potter County. These trips made economical vacations since Chuck was a member of the camp. We would drive up there in summer, but in winter as well to take advantage of the snow. Our boys loved hiking and fishing in the summer, building snow forts and sledding in the winter. They would explore the camp's junk heap, searching for "collectibles." One family story often retold in later years was of the time the boys unearthed an old tire. They rolled it down the mountain slope from the junk heap, an unwise decision since it escaped from them, rolling right across a busy road. Fortunately, it didn't strike any cars, and they never tried anything like that again.

Near the hunting camp were the ruins of Austin Dam, which had burst in 1911, the resulting flood wiping out a town of three thousand, the worst catastrophe in Potter County history. Our boys loved exploring the ruins, climbing a crumbling tower, and clambering through the remains of a large mill that once provided employment for the doomed community. The area remains a favored vacation spot for our sons and their families.

We also spent much time together as an extended family. My parents had provided their children with a loving home, and now they were reaping their reward. All of us loved getting together, and Sunday afternoons at Pop Pop and Baba's house were filled with laughter and comradery. Especially during the summer school break, my sons and my sister's and brother's children would flow back and forth from one home to another, the evenings punctuated by phone calls asking to stay over at Aunt Jean's or Uncle Joe's house.

We frequently vacationed together as an extended family. Since we all homeschooled, our children's activities frequently brought us together with co-op activities and field trips. I remember one year when the children had been studying about the Pilgrims and we all came to Thanksgiving dinner in costume.

We also spent time with family on Chuck's side, though less frequently. Chuck's mother died of breast cancer when Charlie was only three years old, and his father ten years later when our youngest son, Jonathan, was only three, so our sons did not grow up knowing their paternal grandparents well. But in our early years of marriage we'd had a great relationship with them. His mother was a seamstress and sewed my first maternity clothes. His father had a beautiful voice and sang in a barbershop quartet in his earlier years.

Because Charlie was older than his brothers when his paternal grandparents passed away, he had the closest relationship of any of them with Chuck's side of the family. Charlie's favorite memory of visiting Pappy and Grammie Roberts while Chuck's mother was still alive was being served his own bottle of Coke. This was a special treat since we didn't have soda except on special occasions. Charlie had one cousin about the same age on this side of the family—Howie. I can envision them now at age three sitting on Grammie's couch and playing together. In later years there weren't as many opportunities to get together, but when they did, they always enjoyed each other's company.

One minor issue that did arouse my concern was that there were no cousins Charlie's age on my side of the family. He was two years older than the next grandchild, his cousin Travis, followed by his brother Josh and cousin Ben, who were the same age. Both my sister and sister-in-law had sons the same year

Zach was born. And so on through more than a dozen cousins so that at family get-togethers each of our younger sons had plenty of cousins to play with.

Though Charlie had no cousins his age close enough to play with, he was not a complete loner. He had two neighborhood buddies named Ryan and Craig. Craig was an especially close friend, and he had the same initials as Charlie—CR. So the two boys decided that when they grew up they were going to be truck drivers and start a company together called CR Trucking. That never happened, but the two remained good friends even after we moved.

Charlie was actually responsible for our last move as a family in 1989. During all these years, the suburban house and yard and driveway we'd once considered so spacious had grown more and more crowded, especially once it teemed with school activities as well as family. We'd added on a small annex, but even so we were bursting at the seams until I was forced to issue orders that the boys could add no more collections larger than a baseball card to the clutter.

Meanwhile Charlie retained happy memories of the quiet and space he'd enjoyed during his homeschool days at Pop Pop and Baba's. He still seized every opportunity to visit there, especially in good weather when he could hike and fish and explore the woods and creeks that surrounded their property. Charlie was sixteen years old when he came across an advertisement in a *TV Guide* for a model, or "stick," home that could be pre-purchased and erected on any property. The list price was $59,900.

Excitedly, Charlie brought us the *TV Guide*. "Look at this house! We could build it right next to Pop Pop and Baba where they have that trailer house."

The trailer house was a unit my parents had moved onto the four acres they'd purchased from the Amish neighbors right next door. Rented out, it was part of their retirement income. Looking at the picture, I sighed. "Oh, Charlie, this would be wonderful. But the price they advertise is never the reality. There are always other hidden costs, including buying the land to build it on, that would put it well above what we could afford."

Disappointed, Charlie put the advertisement away. But the next time we visited my parents, I walked outdoors with my mother to where I could see the trailer house sitting next door. The view of the woods and fields spreading out all around, the ridge with its pine forest rising behind it, was certainly a perfect setting for a family of four energetic boys.

Not seriously, but with some wistfulness, I said to my mother, "Mom, can you believe Charlie thinks we should sell our house in Lancaster and build one on that lot?"

To my surprise, my mother responded, "And why not?"

Within a short time, my parents had sold us a three-quarter acre lot for an excellent price. Putting our Lancaster house up for sale, we moved in with my parents and began building. What a delight it was to witness Charlie's excitement that we were actually carrying out his suggestion. I recall his energetic involvement in every aspect of the project. From where we stayed with my parents, he was constantly heading over to the construction site to check with the builders and report on the progress. In contrast, his youngest brother, Jon, at this time just six years old, earned the nickname "dirt-ball Jon" for his own energetic interaction with the mounds of dirt!

Our Lancaster house sold quickly, and soon we were able to move into our new home. As the oldest, and the person who'd inspired our beautiful new home, Charlie was permitted first pick of the bedrooms. He chose a front bedroom with three windows that offered a panoramic view of the woods and fields he loved. We settled in just in time for hunting season. Charlie shot his first buck in the woods just below our yard, a thrill for any sixteen-year-old.

We now lived surrounded by Amish farms and for the first time had regular contact with the Amish community, above all, our immediate neighbors. Down the road and around the corner was Jake Stoltzfoos, who'd originally sold my parents their property back in 1973. Next to our own lot were the fields of Jake's son Chris. Directly in front of our house lived Jake's other son, Henry, who ran a woodworking business.

While we did not at that time socialize much, we enjoyed neighborly conversations. A special treat was purchasing strawberries, asparagus, and other fresh fruits and vegetables in season from their produce wagon. I do remember when my boys were older and learning to target shoot that we received a visit from Chris, asking that the boys not practice with clay pigeons over his field, since the cows could get sick munching on the broken clay discs. The boys immediately honored his request, and during all those years, we maintained a friendly relationship with our Amish neighbors.

Another joy for Charlie in particular was a new addition to the family. We were still living with my parents when Chuck brought a puppy home. The stray had wandered into the police precinct, and the officers had dubbed her Shadow because she insisted on following the chief of police all around the office. Charlie immediately fell in love with her. Since my parents had just absorbed six more people into their home, I thought it was too much to ask them to take in a dog as well during four months of construction. But Baba's response to her firstborn grandson was typical: "Every boy needs a dog!"

So we—or rather, Charlie—adopted Shadow. After Charlie graduated from high school, he bought another puppy for himself, a Rottweiler mix he named Suzie after the Siberian husky that had died. The two dogs became his closest companions and accompanied him into his married life.

Our move to Strasburg brought one other significant change to our family life. Throughout the years since Charlie's birth, we'd been actively involved in Saint Leo's Catholic Church in Lancaster. Once we'd moved, our original plan was to continue driving up to Lancaster for services. But the parish leadership informed us we needed to transfer our membership to our new parish. We attended services a few times in the Quarryville parish but didn't find the deep fellowship we'd developed in Lancaster.

Then my parents invited us to visit a fairly new church they were now attending near Strasburg: High View Church of God. We immediately felt welcomed and found the church a great fit for our family. It was here too that we met our dear friends Mike and Delores Hayford, who would later become my co-workers at Sight & Sound Theatre. There was an active youth program, and our boys got involved as well in a Bible quizzing team that competed locally and regionally. Chuck had by this time recommitted his life to God through our couples' Bible study, and we both were experiencing spiritual growth through the solid teaching of God's Word we encountered at High View.

The only one of our sons who felt somewhat left out was Charlie. By the time we were well involved at High View, he was graduating from high school, so he never formed a real connection with the church youth. It didn't seem to be a big issue. We'd always studied God's Word as part of our daily homeschooling routine and attended Sunday school together. I can't say there was never any resistance to this from Charlie or the other boys, because at some point, we established a strict family rule that while you live in our home, you go to church.

To me, this season of life was one of blue skies and calm, sweet breezes. I loved my new home. My sons were growing up strong and intelligent and hardworking. They evidenced love for God and for other people. Still, they were not perfect. The world awaiting them outside the protective walls of our home was not always a kind or safe place. Soon they would be of an age to make choices I could not oversee, to leave home for places where I could not protect them.

I remember sharing my concerns with our pastor at High View: "How do I know just what and how to pray for them?"

He gave me a Scripture passage to look up: Colossians 1:9–13. "Pray this passage for each of your sons," he said. "Every time you come across the pronouns 'you' or 'us,' replace them with the name of one of your sons."

Going home, I opened my Bible to the passage and began reading: *"For this reason, since the day we heard about you, we have not stopped praying for you . . ."*

Stopping, I went back and started the passage again, this time following the pastor's instructions: *"For this reason, since the day we heard about* Charlie, *we have not stopped praying for* Charlie. *We continually ask God to fill* Charlie *with the knowledge of his will through all the wisdom and understanding that the Spirit gives, so that* Charlie *may live a life worthy of the Lord and please him in every way: bearing fruit in every good work, growing in the knowledge of God, being strengthened with all power according to his glorious might so that* Charlie *may have great endurance and patience, and giving joyful thanks to the Father, who has qualified* Charlie *to share in the inheritance of his holy people in the kingdom of light. For he has rescued* Charlie *from the dominion of darkness and brought* Charlie *into the kingdom of the Son he loves."*

When I'd finished praying the passage, I started again, this time in turn filling in the names of my other sons—Josh, Zach, and Jon. This became my regular prayer for each of my sons all through their teen years and into their adult lives. With such a powerful and fervent prayer being raised daily on their behalf to the Creator of all, how could my sons not come to love God as deeply and unquestioningly as I had?

9

Choosing Forgiveness

Be kind and compassionate to one another, forgiving each
other, just as in Christ God forgave you.

—Ephesians 4:32

So how had the boy who had been nothing but loving and loved,
the young man who'd shown so much joy in bringing happiness to his family and others, turned into the monster who had
undeniably committed acts so heinous I could not bring myself
to dwell on them? I slept only a few hours that night, tossing
and turning, my anguish flowing out of me in floods of tears.
Despite Betsy's counsel, I found myself returning again and
again to the day's events, trying to make some sense of them.

*Oh, God, this is so awful! I cannot bear that these girls'
deaths be the end of all this!* I cried heavenward. *However terrible this tragedy, I pray that you will bring something good*

out of it, that you will shine some light in the darkness that is all I can see now. If there is anything at all you can use in this situation to bring glory to you, allow that to be.

We had chosen not to watch or read the news, so new tidbits and endless analysis of Charlie's crimes playing out on the television screen did not reach us over the next several days. But we had seen Charlie's farewell notes he'd scribbled to his wife, Marie, and the children. His letter to Marie was lengthy and rambling. He repeatedly emphasized his love for her and his children and how sorry he was for the choices he'd made and the acts he was about to commit. But even his attempts at explanation made no sense.

He expressed remorse for events he claimed had happened when he was only twelve years old. He spoke of having molested a couple of much younger female relatives, who would have been only three to five years old at the time, and of the guilt and torment that had built up in him through the years until he could suppress it no longer. But the police had already investigated those claims and found no evidence that they had ever happened. The relatives in question had no memories of any such events.

But something must have happened to trigger his assertions. At twelve years old, he was still a child, and a sheltered one. Had there been some incident for which he'd blamed himself and then blown far beyond what had actually happened? Had some evil befallen Charlie himself back then? Had someone hurt him? If so, why had he not come and shared it with us who loved him? Why had he buried hurt and shame away to fester inside?

Whatever the truth, we will have no answers in this lifetime, for the answers died with Charlie.

But the other explanation Charlie's letter offered was even less comprehensible. Our son and his wife, Marie, had suffered the loss of their firstborn daughter, Elise Victoria, only twenty minutes after her premature birth. It had indeed been a tragedy. Looking back now, sifting through the rambling phrases of bitterness and blame in Charlie's letter, I can see that to my son, Elise's death was the culmination of loss that had begun with the deaths of grandparents with whom he'd had a bond our other sons weren't old enough to enjoy; the horrible, lingering end of the Siberian husky, Suzie, for which Charlie blamed himself; and the passing of our family pet Cinnamon.

f His losses were no greater than those countless human beings have experienced. God had given Charlie and Marie three beautiful, healthy children. But according to his letter, he'd allowed bitterness and hatred against God to build up inside him. He saw Elise's death as God's punishment for past transgressions rather than seeing his three living children as God's gifts. And now, he bizarrely thought that taking the precious daughters of families who prayed to the same God would be his revenge on the God he'd chosen to no longer worship, love, or forgive for what he perceived as His offenses against him.

It was not only hatred for God he expressed. He wrote: "I'm filled with so much hate toward myself, toward God, and an unimaginable emptiness."

The one sentence in that letter that brought a small comfort was among the last: "Please tell Mom and Dad and my brothers that I love them."

Oh, my son, how did we not see your pain? Why did you not speak to us? Why did you not share your pain and confusion so that we who loved you could help? How could you let bitterness and hatred so consume you—and yet never express it outwardly by any word or deed that those around you could see or hear? There was another way to deal with loss and pain! Why did you not choose it?

85

Forgiven

By the second day, we'd already had more than one glimpse of that other way. Our neighbor Henry was not the only one of the Amish community who reached out to our family in love and forgiveness. Though we were not watching the news, we'd already received word of the story that was sweeping the media, driving Charlie's terrible actions from the headlines. A group of Amish leaders had walked into the yard of Marie's parents. Every one of them had a family member who had died in the schoolhouse. But they were not there to express rage. They had come to offer forgiveness and their concern for the wife and children and extended family of the shooter. They did not raise fists in fury, but as Henry had done with my husband, they reached to pull Marie's father—the "English" neighbor who for so many years had collected their milk and been part of their lives—into their embrace. Together, fathers and grandfathers of the victims and father-in-law of their killer wept and prayed.

"Amish forgiveness" became a catch phrase for the media in countless TV and print news stories. How could these quaint people dressed in black and driving horse-drawn buggies show such willingness to offer forgiveness to the family of their daughters' murderer, much less the murderer himself? What was it about the Amish lifestyle, belief system, faith that made this possible?

It was certainly not because the Amish were perfect people, as their spokesmen immediately pointed out. It came down to the God they worshiped, a God of forgiveness and love.

"If we will not forgive, how can we be forgiven?" were words expressed over and over again, not only by the families affected, but by the greater Amish community across Lancaster County.

"Forgiveness is a choice," explained another Amish spokesman. "We choose to forgive."

But spouting theology is not so difficult. It was the actions of these Amish families that stunned the outside world. Other Amish had stopped by the Welk home, bringing small gifts to express their forgiveness and love. We too had received further visits from various Amish farmers and businessmen for whom my husband drove. By this time, financial help for the grieving Amish families was flooding into Lancaster County from around the nation. A committee was formed to handle the gifts. The Amish families insisted that part of the funds go to Marie and her children, who had lost husband and father as well as their means of support.

From violence and death, the entire world was now focusing its questions on forgiveness and grace. I had prayed that God would bring something good from this terrible tragedy, shine some light in the darkness of these events. Was this the beginning of it?

One visitor we received very early on the third day was an Amish builder for whom Chuck regularly drove. His cousins Daniel Stoltzfus and John Fisher were the fathers of several of the schoolhouse victims. Daniel was the father of eight-year-old Rachel Ann, who was in intensive care. John was the father of three girls who had been in the schoolhouse. Thirteen-year-old Marian had died. The builder was actually heading later that day to her viewing. Eleven-year-old Barbie Fisher had survived four bullets but was in intensive care, while their younger sister Emma had been the only female student to escape the schoolhouse.

If anyone had reason to want no further contact with us, it was this Amish builder, but he'd stopped by to see how we were doing. His stated reason for dropping in was to ask permission to mow our daughter-in-law Marie's lawn, which he noticed was overgrown. But he was also concerned about Marie's other needs. Did she have the necessary funds for the funeral? Was there anything he could do to help?

He also wanted to let us know that the medical needs of the Amish children, as well as funeral expenses, had been met through donations. He shared, too, some of the events in the schoolhouse we had not yet heard about that survivors had now shared with their parents. He told how as Charlie had been barricading the windows, one of his small hostages, nine-year-old Emma Fisher, had heard a woman's voice call, "Run!" Responding, she'd dashed out of the schoolhouse and gone for help. No one else heard the voice, so the Amish wondered if it might have been an angel.

He told how Charlie had asked the girls to pray for him and how he'd almost changed his mind, telling the girls he was going to give himself up to the police. And how when Charlie instead chose to turn his weapon on the girls, the older daughter of his cousin, thirteen-year-old Marian, had bravely spoken up, trying to protect the younger girls, saying, "Shoot me first." He also shared of Marian's younger sister Barbie, who'd survived being shot four times but insisted she felt no pain. We could only hope that God's mercy had equally protected the others from the agony of their injuries.

One astonishing episode he told us was of a woman who'd been driving down the highway just when the shootings happened. She told of seeing a rainbow stretched over the schoolhouse, though there'd been no rain. She and others took it as a sign of God's protection stretching out angelic wings over these young girls in their hour of suffering.

These stories brought me to tears. At every point, this man expressed his love for our family and forgiveness toward Charlie. His kindness encouraged me to pour out my own pain and sorrow. When he finally got up to leave, he asked, "Is there anything else I can do for you?"

As with every visitor, I shared how brokenhearted I was that our son Zach was refusing to come to the funeral. "Will you please pray for Zach that he will have a change of heart and come to his brother's funeral?"

"Of course," he responded in his soft Amish drawl. Then he added, "Would you like me to give him a call?"

The Amish don't have phones in their homes and resist speaking on them, so this offer took me completely aback. If unexpected, the graciousness of his offer deeply touched me, as I knew how distasteful he found such technology. I finally responded, "Oh, yes, please."

We wrote down Zach's phone number. Later we found out that he did indeed call Zach. Zach was not home at the time, but he left a message on his answering machine, offering his prayers and love and pleading with him to forgive his brother and come home for the funeral.

------◆------◆------◆------

Amish Family Member

When my driver Sam took me to the Robertses' home, I was concerned to see that they were all alone. In contrast, there were thousands by now—media, family, and spectators—gathered at Nickel Mines to be there for the victims' families. My heart was moved because it seemed to me that Chuck and Terri were suffering just as much as the parents of Roberts' victims.

When others challenged me as to why I should feel this way, I answered, "What would be worse? Would you rather have lost a child, or have your son have done something like this?"

It is my belief that more good is going to come out of this sad tragedy than bad. After all, what is the most unjust thing that you can think of? The answer is the crucifixion of our Lord Jesus Christ. And yet what should be the most wonderful thing you can think of? The best thing that has ever happened? Our crucified Savior Jesus Christ rose again.

⟨◆─◆─◆⟩

The funeral itself was the next dreaded hurdle we faced. What funeral home in Lancaster County would want to offer their services for such circumstances as these? Nor did we want to plan services that would conflict with or precede the shooting victims' own laying to rest. We found out that funerals for the five girls were taking place respectively on Thursday and Friday, the third and fourth days after the shooting. In another demonstration of grace and forgiveness, the Amish families had extended an invitation to Marie and her parents, who knew some of these families well, to attend.

So Saturday was chosen for Charlie's funeral. Chuck and I talked over the arrangements with Marie and agreed that the three of us would go together to talk to the local funeral director. By this time, Marie too had called Zach, begging him to come for the sake of his niece and nephews. They needed his support and encouragement and would always remember his absence if he didn't come. As we drove to the funeral home, she shared his resistance with us.

The funeral director told us that at first, he was afraid we might call to request his services for Charlie's funeral. He had the same angry thoughts for Charlie that many carried and didn't want anything to do with his funeral. Then he thought, *I hope they do call. Every family deserves the right to bury their loved ones, even in these circumstances.* Why had he changed his mind? Had he recalled the memory of Charlie's grief-stricken face as our son carried the tiny white coffin that held his firstborn, so

90

small and light Charlie had needed no other pallbearers? This funeral director had been the same who'd officiated over Elise Victoria's services nine years earlier. Apparently, what Charlie had done could not erase the anguish of the loving young father the funeral director had witnessed that day.

I too remembered those tears and the anguish. I had not, I realized suddenly, ever witnessed true, unadulterated joy on my son's face since that terrible day.

I also remembered a time when my son's face could not contain its joy. When the radiance of his happiness overflowed to everyone he encountered.

That was when we realized that our firstborn had fallen in love.

10

Love and Loss

Neither death nor life, neither angels nor demons, neither
the present nor the future, nor any powers, neither height
nor depth, nor anything else in all creation, will be able
to separate us from the love of God that is in Christ Jesus
our Lord.

—Romans 8:38 39

By now our son Josh had managed to catch a flight back from
Louisiana, where he'd been working in the aftermath of Hurricane Katrina. His friend Harry had picked him up from the
airport, and Josh with his wife, Keturah, had immediately
headed over to our home. We'd hugged and cried together.
Now I could see them both outside stretched out on the grass.
Hand in hand, they'd fallen asleep from sheer exhaustion and
grief.

Our youngest son, Jon, and his wife, Megan, had arrived as well. They too looked spent and worn-out. Our sons had always been close. Jon especially had always looked up to Charlie, almost a decade older. Again I found my mind retreating back over the years, searching for any red flag that might offer further explanation for what had happened.

But I could find none. By the time Charlie reached the end of his teens, there was not a person I knew who had a negative word to say about him. While still in high school, he'd volunteered to paint houses for Habitat for Humanity. An accomplished handyman, Charlie spent several evenings fixing a garage door for one of my friends. If anyone needed help, Charlie was at the top of their call list.

Charlie found work as a dishwasher in a restaurant. A co-worker there, Gerald, became his closest friend throughout his teen years. But Charlie still struggled with speaking up, especially among strangers. I remember a trip to Disney World when Charlie was sixteen. One shop crafted personalized belt buckles. Charlie had a design in mind, and he asked me to explain it to the craftsman.

"If you want the buckle, you need to explain how you want it designed," I told him. Charlie managed to lay out his idea for the craftsman and was very proud of how the belt turned out.

An even greater challenge for Charlie was speaking in front of a group. One class in his senior year required that he present a lengthy report in front of about a hundred people. Though it definitely took him out of his comfort zone, seeing the smile on his face as he finished and his clear sense of accomplishment brought joy to this mother's heart. I was bursting with pride the day he was honored for graduation at our church service, our only son to graduate from our home education program, as his brothers chose to graduate from private and public high schools. What a long way Charlie had come from those early years when school had been such misery for him!

After graduation, Charlie began working full-time for a construction contractor. He had not given up his dream to become a truck driver one day. Our youngest son, Jon, recalls Charlie taking him four-wheeling in his first new pickup truck when Jon was about ten years old. It was one of his best "big brother" memories. But I will never forget the scare that truck gave us.

That Sunday morning was cold and the roads were icy. Charlie had participated in a Sunday school illustration using balloons. He'd taken one of the balloons home, and while he was driving, the balloon drifted into his line of vision. As he reached over to push away the balloon, his truck hit an ice patch.

We were driving our own vehicle a few minutes behind him. Suddenly we saw a truck flipped over on the road ahead. I could hardly breathe as I recognized it. Desperately I began praying. Then I saw Charlie walking around the truck. God had answered my prayer. He was unhurt, though the truck was totaled.

Memory of that answered prayer brings confusion. *Why, God, did you answer my prayer? Why did you spare Charlie's life then only to permit this to happen? If you could reach down to protect my son when that truck flipped, why did you not reach down this time to prevent his vehicle from ever reaching that schoolhouse?*

If there is a divine answer, I cannot hear it.

Months after these events, I met Charlie's best friend, Gerald, for lunch. He reminisced about the fun he and Charlie had working together at the restaurant, going to movies, heading to the beach, or just hanging out. He could not remember seeing or hearing anything in Charlie that would have led in the direction my son had ultimately taken. Not long after that, I ran into Charlie's childhood friend Craig, with whom he'd dreamed of

starting CR Trucking Company. Now married with a family
of his own, he too shared fond memories of Boy Scout outings
with Charlie, riding bikes, playing ball, and endless hours of
conversation.

/ I found it reassuring that they too recalled the Charlie of my
own memories. Quiet. Strong. Caring. Honest. Kind. Hardworking. Okay, so I am his mother. But I've found no one who
remembers him differently. If there were troubled thoughts and
bitterness with which my son was wrestling, they were buried
deep. Even his younger brothers, who could evince sibling rivalry
among themselves, saw nothing but good in Charlie.

The bottom line was that no one had anything bad to say
about Charlie. He was simply a nice guy that everyone liked.
As I think back now on how normal life seemed to be in those
years, it still defies comprehension to imagine that Charlie could
come to this.

Throughout the years of raising and homeschooling our sons,
I'd occasionally taken on part-time work, especially when extra
funds were needed. I'd worked at an ice cream store to earn
money for my parents' twenty-fifth anniversary celebration,
at a bank to earn the funds for a car of my own. When our
youngest, Jon, was still homeschooling but no longer needed
constant supervision, I applied at Sight & Sound Theatre for
a position in the concessions department.

I worked in concessions for several years before becoming
the manager for that department. When Sight & Sound Theatre burned down in 1997, I opened my own personal catering
business for funerals, weddings, and parties. But I closed that
business to return to Sight & Sound when the theater reopened. I
eventually worked my way to manager of the food and merchandise areas, the position I held when the Nickel Mines tragedy
occurred. Each of my three younger sons, Josh, Zach, and Jon,

worked for me part-time during their teen years. Zach and Jon worked in my department after the fire. Josh worked full-time on the deck where scenery sets were moved.

I'd loved staying home to raise my sons. But I also enjoyed this new challenge and the interaction with thousands of visitors who traveled from across North America and even overseas to attend the Sight & Sound productions.

Charlie was twenty-one when it became apparent he'd fallen in love. Marie Welk and her family attended our church. Close in age to our third son, Zach, Marie had grown up in the youth programs with our younger sons. When she was only fourteen, she'd been the youngest participant in a youth mission trip to New Mexico in which our second son, Josh, sixteen at the time, had also participated.

While we'd had little personal contact with Marie, we knew her as a sweet girl, highly intelligent, hardworking, and caring. Her father worked in the family business, Welk Milk Hauling, a business founded by Marie's great-grandfather that collected milk from the region's Amish farms and hauled it to several large corporate dairies for processing into pasteurized milk, butter, cheese, yogurt, and ice cream. Even in high school, Marie worked in her family's business. A talented pianist, Marie also had a beautiful voice and sang in the choir. She taught Sunday school and helped with the little ones. She was altogether the kind of young lady of whom any mother with four sons would approve.

For several years leading up to this point, my mother had been working on a play she'd titled *The Way of War*, centered on the life she'd lived growing up in Columbia, Pennsylvania, during World War II. Her sister Clare had written songs to adapt the play into a musical. The play was eventually sponsored for production as a cultural event in Columbia. A number of my mother's many grandchildren were in the cast. The play proved a great success, selling out several shows with an audience of more than two hundred each.

/ At this time Marie was seventeen years old and in her junior year of high school. Charlie was twenty-one. Marie had been asked to play the role of a war-time nurse in the play. Charlie was to have played the role of a soldier. Because of his shyness in front of crowds, he chose in the end to work the ticket stand. However, by that time, he'd already made the *Lancaster Sunday News* in full military uniform as part of a cast photo.

When the production ended, my mother threw a cast party at her home for everyone involved in the production. Though Marie and Charlie attended the same church, they had not really interacted, since Charlie was four years older and out of the youth program. If Charlie was shy, Marie was beautiful, confident, and serene. Charlie could not keep his eyes off of her. He found her easy to talk with, and she in turn seemed to enjoy his dry humor and sweet smile.

At the end of the evening, Marie announced that she needed to leave. Standing up, my mother said, "I'll walk you to the door."

Uncharacteristically, Charlie put his leg out, blocking his grandmother. Touching her arm, he said, "I'll take care of that."

Walking over to Marie, he asked with his quiet smile, "Do you mind if I walk you to your car?"

Marie consented. By the time she drove away, Charlie had asked her for a date. The two dated for the rest of Marie's high school years. I remember the first time Charlie brought her home to dinner at our house. She brought a pretty blue heart ornament to hang on the wall. I remember Charlie taking Marie to the prom and how proud he looked to be with this beautiful girl in a gorgeous pink dress, the girl of his dreams.

Quiet though he was, he could not keep his joy to himself. I listened as he bubbled over about his happiness that Marie cared so much for him, about how easy she made it for him to talk. Marie's older brother, Ken, was close in age to Charlie, the Welk home similar to ours in values and background and with a strong, loving family bond. He was soon spending as much time there as at home. When he wasn't with Marie, he was spending hours on the phone talking to her. Never had I seen my firstborn so happy or open in communication.

At Christmas, during Marie's senior year of high school, Charlie and Marie announced their engagement. Charlie had first asked her father's permission to propose. The Welks had given their warm approval, welcoming Charlie as a second son. For our part, Marie was the kind of daughter we had always wanted.

That next fall, on November 9, 1996, Charlie and Marie exchanged their vows in a beautiful wedding at High View Church of God. Charlie's face beamed with pride and joy as Marie's unique voice rose in song to him during the ceremony.

The young couple had found a place to live in the small town of Lititz, about forty minutes' drive from both the Welks and us, but near Marie's Aunt Linda and Uncle Jim. The small house had needed lots of repairs to make it livable, but with Charlie's handyman skills and Marie's flair for interior design, they made it a beautiful home. Charlie continued working in house construction, and Marie found work with a health-care company. We saw less of them since they now lived beyond an easy drop-in, but when we did, their patent joy and contentment made all of us smile.

Two months before Charlie and Marie's wedding, our second son, Josh, married his high school sweetheart, Laura, whom he too had met in the youth program at High View. Our third son,

Zach, had finished film school in Florida and was working in New York. Our fourth son was enjoying his high school years. I in turn was delighting in my job. Life was good. I had succeeded in my greatest life goal—raising four sons to be good, loving, hardworking young men.

Neither Charlie nor Marie wanted to wait to start their own family. It was around Father's Day when they shared the news that Marie was expecting a child, her due date sometime in February. Not long after, Josh and Laura shared that they too would be parents in March. How excited we were to find out we'd be grandparents. How much more happiness could life hold?

But the calm, sweet tenure of our life was interrupted in September when Marie began having difficulties with the pregnancy. After a frightening episode when it seemed she would lose the baby, Marie was confined to bed rest for the remainder of her pregnancy. But just after Charlie and Marie's first anniversary, three months still before her due date, Marie went into labor. On November 14, 1997, baby Elise Victoria was born, perfectly formed and beautiful, but only 12¼ inches long and just over one pound in weight. Charlie and Marie had twenty sweet minutes with her before her life returned to the God who had formed her in her mother's womb.

There was a quiet service for baby Elise Victoria's funeral. Charlie and Marie wept together. All the joy of these last two years was gone from Charlie, his face pallid and somber as he carried the tiny white casket to the hearse for the drive to the cemetery.

But within a few days, Charlie was back hard at work. As was his pattern, he spoke little of his loss, at least not to parents and friends. We prayed that he and Marie would find healing together. Marie returned to work. A few months later in March, our granddaughter Maddi was born. Charlie and Marie expressed only joy for Josh and Laura, but we knew it had to be hard for them to see this healthy baby girl and Josh and Laura's happiness.

It was about a year after Elise's death when Marie learned that she was pregnant again. This time we saw little joy in Charlie, only worry that this baby too would be taken from them. And sure enough, within a few weeks baby Isabelle joined her sister Elise Victoria in heaven. To make matters worse, the doctors expressed concerns that the difficulties of this miscarriage might make it unlikely for Marie to get pregnant again.

Though Charlie was quieter than usual, that dry sense of humor and sweet, impish smile rarely showing itself, he insisted all was well. Should I have talked to my son more about his sorrow? Would it have made a difference? Again, there is no way now to know. And Charlie made it clear he found no benefit in discussing his grief over events that could not be changed. When we were together as a family, it was hardly unusual for Charlie to spend more time listening to his siblings' joys and activities than speaking of his own.

Then in early 1999, Charlie and Marie shared with us that Marie was again pregnant. Despite the loss and grief Marie too had endured, we'd seen her faith in God grow. She shared how God had spoken to her heart that she would bear a healthy baby girl. She'd already been given the name for this yet unborn child.

Charlie was less convinced. He worried that this pregnancy would end like the others. But on September 2, 1999, Marie gave birth to a beautiful baby girl. Only twenty-two months later she had a baby brother.

By this time Charlie and Marie had moved back to our area, building a modular home on a lot next door to Marie's grandparents and just a few minutes' walk from her parents' home in Georgetown. Charlie had also realized his own personal dream of becoming a trucker. Marie's father, Ken, who had always treated Charlie as a second son, mentored him and trained him on one of his own eighteen-wheelers until Charlie passed the test to get his trucking license.

From that point on, Charlie started working for the Welk Milk Hauling Company. The schedule of milking meant that he worked a night shift, leaving home after his children were in bed and getting back in the early morning hours. His route each night from one dairy farm to another put him in contact with many of the farming families in southern Lancaster County's Amish community.

To all appearances, Charlie had by now recovered from the grief of losing two daughters. Still quiet, he smiled more, especially when playing with his children. His deep love for his children, and for Marie, was evident. He spoke openly about how much he enjoyed his new job. Though he worked long hours, he always had time for family—not only for Marie and his children, but for family get-togethers at our home or with Marie's parents, or going to the beach or hunting or just seeing a movie with his brothers. After Charlie's death, I searched through my photo albums to find a good picture of him. But I couldn't find a single snapshot of just Charlie. Every picture showed him surrounded by family.

If there was one lack I can see now from a rearview perspective, it was that Charlie did not appear to carry any deep friendships into his married life. His best friend from high school, Gerald, was not married and had other interests. By this time Chuck and I had begun to attend a daughter church that High View had planted a few years earlier—Living Faith Church of God. Since moving close by, Charlie and Marie had begun attending there as well. But we didn't see Charlie forming any close relationships with other men in the church.

I didn't see this as unusual, since having a wife and family takes a young man in a different direction than when his life centers around friends and the social activities of single life. When he was present, Charlie showed no difficulties interacting with family, friends, and co-workers, joining in their comradery, if rarely initiating his own. By now his two dogs Suzie and Shadow had died, but Charlie and Marie had purchased the yellow Lab puppy they named Dale, and Charlie enjoyed training the dog and spending time with him.

When he needed alone time, Charlie still found relaxation tinkering with anything that could be taken apart and put together. A major hobby was trying to restore an old jeep he'd acquired. He finally managed to get the engine running, but it never got out on the road due to other mechanical issues.

For my part, I was deeply thankful that my firstborn had found contentment in marriage, fatherhood, work, and hobbies. After a season of storms, he and his young family had found shelter at least for this season in a safe, calm harbor. I could stop worrying about Charlie.

What did I miss? I was—will always be—his mother! Surely if anyone could spot signs of trouble, it would be the woman who gave him birth. At what point did bitterness begin to seethe beneath the surface contentment? Or hate tug harder at the mind and heart than love?

I saw nothing. But my attention was elsewhere.

By this time I was clutching tightly to normalcy with clawing, desperate fingertips in the midst of a hurricane.

11

Hurricane

The cords of the grave coiled around me; the snares of death confronted me. In my distress I called to the LORD; I cried to my God for help.

—Psalm 18:5–6

If I thanked God that my firstborn had found a calm harbor, it was because we were going through more troubled waters with the rest of our family. Our second son, Josh, and his wife, Laura, had still been in their teens when they married. They'd moved out to New Mexico by the time their daughter Maddi was born. But she was only three years old when their marriage ended in divorce, a devastating time for our son and the whole family.

Meanwhile, after graduating from film school in Florida, our son Zach had followed his dream of film production to

New York. But he hadn't been able to find work in that field and was having to take on any job he could find to pay bills. Neither Josh nor Zach could afford to come home often. Our youngest son, Jon, had moved to Lancaster City once he was out of high school, and though he dropped by now and then, his social circle was now his own set of friends.

In November 2002, Josh called to let us know he'd be having knee surgery. He would also be spending his first Thanksgiving alone. My heart broke for him. I called my own mother, and the two of us made plans to fly to New Mexico, where we could give Josh the support of family during his surgery and cook him a good Thanksgiving dinner before flying home.

The evening before our flight, I was still organizing my packing when the phone rang. It was my doctor's office. I'd gone in a short time earlier for a routine mammogram. They would not be wasting a phone call if the results were my usual clean bill of health, so immediately my stomach tensed. The caller had no specific results for me, only said that something suspicious had shown up on the X ray. "You need to make an immediate appointment with an oncologist."

I wasn't as surprised as I might have been. In the short time since the mammogram, I'd noticed an unusual black-and-blue bruising around the examination area, far more so than with any previous mammogram. Already my mind was conjuring up scenarios. A fatty cyst? Benign tumor? Cancer?

But I could not let myself even go there. At this point my son's need took priority. I didn't even consider canceling my flight. *I'll deal with this when I get home*, I told myself firmly. *Right now my only focus is Josh.*

I did share the news with Chuck. We decided together not to mention the phone call until after Mom and I returned from New Mexico. The last thing I wanted was for my mother or anyone else in the family to be worrying about me during this difficult time in Josh's life.

But keeping my fears tamped down and a smile on my face wasn't easy. Josh's surgery was successful. My mother and I stayed in New Mexico for about a week. We cooked up an elaborate Thanksgiving dinner. Our visit had been a good one, and I'd been reasonably successful at banishing from my thoughts all the possibilities that phone call implied. But one day as I was dressing, my mother walked into the room in time to catch sight of the bruising on my chest, now even uglier in its black-and-blue mottling. Shocked, she demanded to know what was wrong. It was a relief to share my fears and to pray together.

Once back in Lancaster County, I called immediately to make an appointment. But it was mid-December before I was able to meet with the doctor. Despite my misgivings, I drove to the oncologist's office with an optimistic attitude. For one, I believe · in a God who wants the best for us. I trusted that God held my future in His hands. I never once asked, "Why me?" On the contrary, I knew well that I was no different from anyone else, and countless millions faced health crises every year. So why *not* me?

But by the time the oncologist explained the results, I was stunned. The X ray not only showed a large tumor, but the diagnosis was inflammatory breast cancer, stage three (IBC). I quickly learned that IBC is considered one of the most aggressive cancers because it grows so quickly, is often widespread at the time of discovery, and is more likely to come back after treatment than other types of breast cancer.

The oncologist laid out the course of treatment ahead of me, which included eight rounds of chemotherapy followed by a radical mastectomy. She explained also how sick the treatment would make me, with loss of hair, nausea, and weakness beyond the devastation of the surgery itself.

I left her office feeling far less optimistic. I stopped at the reception desk to make my follow-up appointments and waited while the receptionist made a phone call to set up my schedule with the surgeon. I'll never forget my feeling of disbelief when the receptionist referred to me on the phone as a "C-patient."

That's not me! I told myself, stunned. *I'm a healthy person. I've always been a healthy person.* It felt like an out-of-body experience.

But in reality, I now had a new identity. I was a cancer patient. If all went well and God showed mercy, someday I would be a cancer survivor. But cancer would always be part of my identity from this day forward.

My next appointment was with the surgeon. Medical personnel are usually pretty expressionless when dealing with patients. But I caught a look of aghast disbelief on the surgeon's face as she took in the unsightly discoloration of my bruises and then quickly turned her eyes away. She picked up the X ray to examine it. I'd been counseled to take along a voice recorder to my various appointments. Listening now to the recording I took during that appointment, I can hear again the sharp emphasis of her exclamation, "This tumor is *so* large!"

Her commentary should have scared me to death. This storm had blown into my life so completely out of the blue. Of all the disasters that could have befallen me, this was one that had simply never crossed my mind. Just how much was my life about to change?

If my worst fears had just been confirmed, I also felt peace. Perhaps to some degree I was still in shock. Maybe I just hadn't quite grasped how deadly a prognosis stage three IBC implied. Or how few survived long-term to tell the tale. But at the same time I had confidence that God was in control of my life and that He could bring healing.

/ A major encouragement was a friend of mine named Johanna, who had also been diagnosed with breast cancer that had in time become lung cancer. She'd been told she had only three months to live. Along with traditional medicine, she'd chosen to pursue an alternative cancer treatment called the "living foods diet." It is based on Genesis 1:29–30, where God says, "I give you every seed-bearing plant . . . and every tree that has fruit with seed in it . . . I give every green plant for food."

Practically speaking, this translated into giving up meat, dairy, processed flour, sugar, and similar foods and eating only freshly harvested plants, seeds, nuts, legumes, etc. Since I thoroughly enjoyed the traditional German/Irish foods we prepared as a family, I'd had no interest in joining my friend's new lifestyle. But one major downside of chemotherapy is that it doesn't only kill cancerous cells, but kills healthy ones as well. The proponents of living foods claimed that this diet, first given to Adam and Eve by God himself in the Garden of Eden, was not only healthier, but restored the human body's own natural healing ability, strengthening its immune system to fight off infection and disease.

These claims had certainly proved true for Johanna, who was still alive and healthy eight years after being given three months to live. She urged me to visit Optimum Health Institute, the holistic healing center in Southern California that had helped her shift her eating and exercise habits. I wasn't quite ready to take such a drastic step. Instead I started chemotherapy, but I did begin a modified version of Johanna's living foods diet.

"If the chemo and surgery don't work," I told Johanna, "I'll consider going all the way with your program."

I began chemotherapy and the new diet on the same day. Others with whom I shared my plan thought I was crazy. They insisted I needed meat protein to keep up my strength. Within five days I was feeling so ill at work that it seemed clear to me the new diet was not helping. Heading home, I opened a can of chicken and made a chicken salad sandwich. After gobbling it down, I felt so much better that I decided the naysayers had been right about not giving up meat protein.

When I shared my experience with Johanna, she reassured me that detoxifying the body of animal products and processed foods can make you feel ill for a few days, but that it would pass. In any case, the chicken hadn't helped. Almost immediately, I was feeling even worse than before. I could actually taste the effects of the chemo—a strong metallic taste, like chewing on nickels. And my mouth was filled with ulcers.

I returned to the modified living foods diet, but over the next months, I lost not only my hair, but my fingernails, toenails, even my eyelashes. I was so weak I could hardly function. In the context of everything else, perhaps it seems trivial, but I felt so ugly! My beauty pageant days were long gone, but I'd always taken pride in a good appearance. Now I couldn't bear to look at myself in the mirror.

Even in this, I sought to find humor. One week toward the end of my chemo, our church was sponsoring a coffeehouse with skits and other wholesome comedy entertainment. One of the skits being prepared involved eight bald men. I said to the organizer of the skit, "Hey, would you like another volunteer? I've lost all my hair!"

He looked at me skeptically. "Are you kidding? Would you really do that?"

"Sure, why not!" I assured him.

So out on the stage that night walked seven bald men—and one bald woman. The skit itself was hilarious, and the audience responded to my lines with roars of laughter. Afterward, a number of church members approached me to say how much they'd appreciated my participation: "Thank you for bringing into the open this whole issue of cancer. We've wanted to express our sympathy. We just didn't know what to say."

Through this time, I continued working. While friends and co-workers commented on my positive outlook, there were times in the dark hours of the night when fear would creep in, stealing away the sleep I so desperately needed. Throughout, I was comforted by the outpouring of prayer on my behalf from family, friends, and my church.

Another comfort was Scripture. I'd begun memorizing verses when I first started Neighborhood Bible Studies. Now I found myself turning to certain passages to calm me when fears arose or when I was feeling particularly ill after a chemo session. One of these was Philippians 4:6–7:

> Do not be anxious about anything, but in every situation, by prayer and petition, with thanksgiving, present your requests to God. And the peace of God, which transcends all understanding, will guard your hearts and your minds in Christ Jesus.

It was a passage I'd heard and read often enough over the years, but its meaning had never really struck home—perhaps because I hadn't needed it like I did now. A particular phrase jumped out at me: "Do not be anxious . . . but in every situation . . . *with thanksgiving*, present your requests to God."

I'd poured out my anxious fears and petitions to God often enough. But I'd never really noticed the command to offer those petitions *with thanksgiving*. Once God healed me, there'd certainly be reason to give thanks. But what was there to give thanks about in the midst of such a desperate situation? I began to pray.

Thank you, heavenly Father, for that mammogram showing this tumor before it was too late. Thank you for access to good doctors. Thank you for such wonderful support from loving family and friends. Thank you for employers who are always understanding when I'm feeling sick from chemo. Thank you that my life is in your hands. Thank you for surrounding me with your love.

Yes, there was indeed reason to give thanks, no matter what my current circumstances. When I could think of nothing else to pray, I would turn to more Scripture passages I'd memorized. Always they brought comfort.

If you are going through trials, if the way seems dark ahead, if the winds and waves of life's storms are crashing around you until you feel you are drowning, I cannot recommend strongly enough the value of committing God's Word to your heart and mind through memorization. Then, whether alone in the dark of a sleepless night, driving your vehicle, or taking a walk, you can simply speak out to God the promises He has given in His Word. With every petition, thank God for the blessings He has brought into your life (and if you search, you will find many, even if they are simply clean water to drink and food on your table!). As you do so, I guarantee that you will, like me, encounter God's peace replacing fear and anxiety in your heart and mind.

Find something to be thankful for!

12

Calm Waters

He reached down from on high and took hold of me;
he drew me out of deep waters. . . . The LORD was my
support.

—Psalm 18:16–18

Once the rounds of chemo were finished, my surgery was set
for early May 2003. I came through it without any major com-
plications, and it was with great optimism that I went in for
my follow-up appointment. I'd put up uncomplainingly with
a considerable amount of physical suffering. I'd maintained a
positive attitude and expressed openly my faith in God's ability
to heal. At that moment I had absolutely no doubt that my faith
was about to be rewarded. The oncologist would let me know
that between the surgery and the chemo, the cancer cells were
now gone. I could begin life again with a clean slate.

113

But the oncologist's briefing held no such good news. A radical mastectomy had removed the cancer, but seven out of eleven of my lymph nodes were affected. Recommended treatment involved more chemo plus radiation and a five-year cancer drug regimen.

My first appointment with the radiologist was the following Monday. Chuck offered to go with me, but I insisted I was fine. It would just be an in-and-out visit. Then I'd head on over to my job at Sight & Sound Theatre. But when I met with the radiologist, he informed me that in order to target the affected lymph nodes, the radiation would also target—and damage—much of the healthy lung tissue underneath.

I was devastated to hear that more damage would be done to my already ravaged body. My surgical incisions needed attention, so from the radiologist's office, I stopped in to see the surgeon. While she was dealing with my drainage, I asked her flat out, "So what are we talking about as far as my life expectancy?"

Her response was just as straightforward: "Looking at these results, there is now at best a 50 percent chance you'll be alive in five years."

These were not the statistics I'd been waiting to hear. Nor was this in the plan I'd been so sure God had for my life. All the strength and determination with which I'd endured chemo and surgery left me that day. For the first time I questioned whether I would live through this. Were my hope and expectation of God's healing a reality to which I should cling, or just some fantasy with which I'd been deluding myself?

God, what is your plan for me? I cried out as I drove back to work at Sight & Sound. Tears streamed down my face. *I believed you were going to heal me. This was not the news I was expecting!*

Faith is not faith unless it is tested. In my despair, I clung to the one reality of which I had no doubt. My heavenly Father, who had created me, who had healed my son in my womb, who had made known His love for me since my earliest childhood, also held my future in His almighty hand. Whatever choice He made for my life and future, it would be the right one.

It was then that I remembered my promise to Johanna. Following her lead was not as simple as adding the living foods lifestyle she followed to the traditional treatment of radiation, chemo, and drugs that the oncologist had recommended. Traditional treatment killed healthy cells as well as sick ones. This alternative promised to stimulate my body's own healing abilities to overcome the sick cells with healthy ones. But that necessitated *not* killing off the healthy cells. I would have to commit to one course of treatment or the other. If I chose wrongly, the consequence could mean my life.

I prayed for wisdom. Then I picked up the phone. At least I could check out the program Johanna was recommending. I called my husband first. "Would you mind if I flew to California for three weeks?"

He knew exactly what I was referring to. His calm answer came immediately: "You do what you have to do."

My next call was to the Optimum Health Institute (OHI). The staff I dealt with on the phone were warm and reassuring. They would be able to book me into their Southern California facility as early as that next Sunday. I immediately booked a flight. My mother, always my staunch supporter, volunteered to travel with me. I asked my family, friends, and church to pray with me for wisdom in making decisions.

Optimum Health Institute's Southern California campus proved to be an oasis of peace and quiet on the outskirts of San Diego, its Spanish-style buildings with white walls and red-tiled roofs sprawled among green lawns, bright flower beds, and palm trees. Relaxation, fellowship, excellent teaching, and exercise made the regimen feel like a summer retreat.

Getting used to the food was less pleasurable. The detoxification program began with a three-day juice fast, followed by a diet of only living foods—vegetables, grains, sprouts, wheat grass juice. Since I was on a cancer regimen, even fruits were proscribed at this point. One positive side effect was that the program also proved an effective weight loss diet, something I certainly counted as a bonus.

But my mother was not in need of weight loss. She not only found the food unpalatable, but within a few days she'd lost so much weight her own health was in jeopardy. At my insistence, she reluctantly headed home to Lancaster County. But to my delight, my friend Delores immediately insisted on flying out to take her place.

I spent a total of three weeks at OHI. My interlude there proved not only a time of physical healing, but also of spiritual renewal. Marie had sent me off with a CD she'd put together of encouraging Scriptures and music. What a blessing this was as I listened to it over and over. After the first week, Delores and I began a daily Bible study with some of the other women. As we studied God's promises in Scripture and shared both the challenges and blessings illness had brought into our lives, I felt peace like sweet, gentle rain bringing new life to my thirsty soul.

The strict diet and gentle exercise were also restoring life to my battered physical frame. During the months of chemotherapy, not only had my body lost every hair, fingernail, and toenail, but I'd also been stripped of all my strength. Now I could feel health returning to my body. How excited I was when my hair began to grow back. I drank in the practical instruction that could help me maintain this new lifestyle once I returned home.

One day as my friend Delores and I were reading our Bibles, she read aloud the Scripture passage in 1 Corinthians 3:16: "Don't you know that you yourselves are God's temple and that God's Spirit dwells in your midst?"

Delores looked over at me. "I always thought I'd taken good care of my temple because I don't drink or smoke." I saw tears in her eyes as she added, "I now realize I wasn't caring for God's temple at all."

I understood what she meant. When the car we depend on to get us safely from one place to another starts making a strange noise, or the engine light comes on, we immediately address the problem. Why? Because we know that if we ignore the issue, sooner or later our vehicle is no longer going to get us where we want to go. But when our bodies send us a signal that something is wrong, we try to cover up the warning signal with a pill. Too often we don't want to bother dealing with the underlying reason the warning has come.

I was still wrestling with the question of continuing treatment for the cancer. I'd come here to investigate the pros and cons. But I'd soon have to make a choice—whether to embrace the program or make an appointment with the radiologist. During one of the class sessions at OHI, I was asked what I was most afraid of. I answered honestly that I wasn't afraid to die. But I *was* afraid of making a wrong decision.

If I chose OHI's natural healing route and two years later died of cancer, would my family be angrily asking why I had rejected traditional treatment? On the other hand, if I submitted to radiation, chemo, and drugs, and in two years the oncologist's grim prognosis became a reality, would my grieving family be questioning why I hadn't been courageous enough to try this alternative? Either way, the wrong choice would leave my loving husband, sons, and grandchildren prematurely and unnecessarily without a wife, mom, and grandmother. This experience became my "light-bulb moment." I knew what God's plan was for me: I would continue to pursue this healthy lifestyle 100 percent.

Only wisdom from God could help me make the right choice. In all of this, my faith was growing—not in the new living foods lifestyle, though I could already feel renewed strength. My faith was in God, who had brought me through this challenge. He had become my rock, my sanctuary, my firm foundation in the midst of this hurricane. As long as my focus remained on Him, this storm would not sweep me away, no matter how raging the tempest became.

My decision to stick with the OHI program came at the end of the three weeks. Beyond any shadow of doubt, I knew that I knew that I knew that living foods was God's leading for my life. For *my* life, I want to emphasize, because every health crisis and every life journey is different. I would never presume to say that God's leading should be the same for every person.

Flying back to Lancaster County, I headed to the health foods store and farmer's market instead of my radiologist. I never went back for any further chemo, surgery, or drugs. Instead, I followed faithfully the regimen OHI had laid out for me. When my follow-up tests came back six months later, it was my oncologist's turn to express disbelief. The tests revealed no cancer cells at all!

To this day, I continue to follow a living foods diet. Year after year, I have returned for my annual wellness checkup with my oncologist, only to be given an "all clear." What healed me? Traditional medicine? The living foods lifestyle? God's healing touch on my body?

I have no doubt all three played a role.

I felt that I could now understand God's purpose in allowing the hurricane of cancer to shake up my life. My new passion was to help others with the help I had received. I had never been comfortable speaking in front of a large group. But I could invite others to my home to share God's healing power, both supernatural and natural, through the discoveries of science and medicine God has made possible.

Soon my house was filling up with cancer patients and people with other health problems interested in my journey of faith and the benefits I'd experienced from the living foods lifestyle. Chuck was patient with the influx of visitors. But they quickly became so many that I cut back to a support group every third Monday of the month. There was no organized program. I simply let it be known that I would be home that evening to share my story and answer any questions.

That became a ritual that continues to this day. Some months, twenty or more people would show up. Sometimes it might be just two or three. Church and community groups also began inviting me to share my story. In time, I grew more comfortable with public speaking. How exciting to hear in turn, as the months passed, stories from those who'd attended of how the living foods lifestyle had changed their lives and brought healing.

Even more exciting was to discover over time that I'd not only recovered the health I'd known before the cancer diagnosis, but a far greater measure. At my age, I'd battled a number of small ailments common enough to this season of life, from a toxic liver to acid reflux, arthritis, and dry eye syndrome. All of these had disappeared since I'd begun the living foods lifestyle. In fact, I was experiencing an energy and vitality I hadn't known since my twenties and thirties.

Wow, life is great! I kept telling myself with astonishment. *While others complain about growing older, I'm getting healthier.*

During one of my annual follow-ups several years later, I asked my oncologist why she and other oncologists were so reluctant to include the living foods program in their list of treatment options. "You've seen what it's done in my life. How can you not at least offer it as an alternative for your other patients?"

As always, her answer was straightforward: "It's simple. At least 80 percent of my patients would opt for your program. But of that 80 percent, I could count on less than 40 percent follow-through. This worked for you because you committed yourself to the program 110 percent. If they don't follow through with the lifestyle changes, patients will be worse off than with chemo and other traditional treatments. At least with chemo and drugs, I can be sure of the documented benefits."

I couldn't disagree with her. The living foods lifestyle had transformed my life. But it is not an easy program to follow. Comfort foods are very addictive. Many who've tried simply cannot give up the salty, fatty, meaty foods they love even for the sake of extending their lives.

But I am so thankful today I didn't allow worries or questions to keep me from getting on that plane. May I encourage you who are reading this book never to be afraid of allowing God to expand your horizons as long as your faith walk is strong in Him.

By 2006, I'd been cancer-free for more than a year. The past months had been filled with blessing for our family. In the spring of 2005, Charlie and Marie welcomed another healthy baby boy. By then Josh had moved back to Lancaster County. In June 2005, he married a beautiful young woman, Keturah. In November 2005, the whole family gathered again for our youngest son Jon's marriage to Megan. As much as I loved my four sons, I'd always longed for a daughter. Now I had three beautiful, loving daughters-in-law.

But our sons were also busy now with their own families. I remember a family trip to Hershey Park in December to see the Christmas lights. That same winter, Zach came for a visit from New York. We all met for dinner at Olive Garden restaurant. Even Baba and Pop Pop were with us. I remember the laughter and teasing between my sons, Charlie joining in as much as anyone.

My son Josh shares one of his favorite memories of that year. He was hunting deer with Charlie when they spotted a black bear just twenty yards down the mountainside. The two young men hunkered down to watch the bear dig grubs out of a log and pop them into its cavernous mouth until darkness fell and they had to leave. It remains a special last memory for Josh of his big brother.

But overall, we did get together less often. We'd always taken a joint family vacation. This year we could not find a date that would work for everyone, and we finally enjoyed a camping trip with those who could make it instead of our mountain vacation. Perhaps because I didn't spend as much time with Charlie, I never picked up on any red flags, except to notice a bit of sadness once in a while.

For me, life had returned to its normal pleasant calm. I'd learned to give thanks in the midst of the hurricane. Now I could praise God the hurricane was at last over. God had restored my life and health. He'd granted me joy and purpose in helping others with the same help I'd received.

So I felt only thankfulness and anticipation as I boarded a plane once again, this time to Toulouse, France. Our friends Chuck and Cathy Powers, who'd been so helpful when we started homeschooling, had been serving as missionaries in Toulouse for almost two decades.

I thank God that in His mercy He allowed me no warning that the hurricane I'd just survived was only the mildest of precursors to the tsunami poised to engulf my life.

13

A Garment of Praise

Provide for those who grieve . . . the oil of joy instead of mourning, and a garment of praise instead of a spirit of despair.

—Isaiah 61:3

The media were relentless.

We'd grown accustomed to seeing their white logoed vans, clusters of boom microphones, and cameras anytime we stepped outside. Yes, they were doing their jobs. But their implacable hovering was as annoying—and fortunately as easily shooed aside—as clouds of gnats in summertime.

Still, I could not remain resentful of their persistence because it was through the media that grace entered our household in a way we had never expected. From the first day we'd experienced support from family, friends, and church. We'd been lifted up and comforted by their prayers. People brought meals to us. I was especially touched by those who'd gone out of their way to make up raw, organic, vegan meals for my special diet.

But when cards and letters began to pour in from around the country, I cringed. What could these strangers have to say to Chuck and me, the parents of a mass murderer? With the stories that had played out on the news, what outpourings of recrimination and hatred lay inside the sealed flaps of these envelopes?

When I finally mustered the courage to skim through the mound of mail, I was stunned by its contents. Far from angry outpourings, the letters were filled with compassion and love. Some expressed sorrow for our loss. Others shared of going through similar pain with a prodigal child. They spoke of hearts touched by the theme of forgiveness this story had made public. All emphasized prayer for us. Prayers for Marie and the children. Prayers for the Amish families grieving their lost daughters.

We also received a number of prayer shawls from individuals and churches. There were so many, in fact, that we passed some on as gifts to bless others. Knowing that the women who'd crocheted or knitted these shawls had prayed for us as they worked was warmth to my soul. I was not just wrapping intricately woven yarn around me, but a covering of caring and intercession.

Raw emotions still ebbed and flowed like waves crashing over me so that at moments I felt I could not endure one more pain-filled breath. But as I read those letters and cards, as I wrapped a prayer shawl around me, I felt the comforting embrace of countless warm, loving arms. More so, I felt the keen awareness of prayer rising around the world to blanket this small piece of Lancaster County with grace and love and forgiveness like the gentle touch of a down-filled Amish quilt.

Excerpts From Cards

What can I say to you that a hundred people haven't already said? I just want you to know how I hurt for you. I would never try to say I know all you are going through, but I do know the heartache of losing a son. Nothing I can say will make it better. Just know I am thinking of you and praying for you.

—Author unknown

Stay focused on Him and His power and presence, and you will continue to walk on the water. I'm praying and believing that you will sense God's presence and peace like never before.

—Kate

May peace like a river attend your soul in the coming months and years.

—Handmade card from Japanese students
Ryoko, Yukika, Rieko, and Karin

Always cherish the memories of your son, and never waver in your faith.

—A teenage family friend

Even though some time has passed, I just wanted to let you know that you are still in my thoughts and prayers. . . . My heart breaks for what you have gone through. I know words that are meant to help can also hurt, so I won't even try to express myself, but I had to thank you for being an inspiration to me and also just let you know that others care about you and are praying for you. God bless you always and forever. Most sincerely, a friend.

—Author unknown

I spent much time myself that week in prayer for the grieving families, especially Thursday and Friday as five young daughters were laid to rest in Bart Township's Amish cemetery. By now I knew well the names of each little girl who'd been in that schoolhouse.

The oldest, Marian Fisher, age thirteen, who asked to be shot first. Her younger sisters Barbie, age eleven, who survived four gunshot wounds, and little Emma, age nine, who so miraculously escaped.

Naomi Rose Ebersol, age seven, and Anna Mae Stoltzfus, age twelve, who died before help could arrive.

Mary Liz Miller, age eight, and Lena Miller, age seven, sisters who survived long enough to be taken to two separate hospitals. Their parents, Chris and Rachel Miller, arrived in time to hold Mary Liz before she died, then had to drive seventy miles to be with Lena, who lived only a few hours longer than her big sister.

Rachel Ann Stoltzfus, age eight, Sarah Ann Stoltzfus, age eight, and Esther King, age thirteen, were all in intensive care but recovering from their wounds.

Rosanna King, age six, had also survived, but endured such massive brain injuries that the doctors didn't know if she'd ever awake from her coma.

While Ken and Nadine Welk, who knew personally several families of the victims, had been invited to their funerals, Chuck and I had not been. Nor would we have wanted our presence to be a reminder of their pain. But we joined each scheduled funeral in thought and prayer. As my prayers rose, I could picture the familiar scene of an Amish funeral so a part of Lancaster County's cultural landscape. The long black line of horse-drawn buggies. Orange traffic cones blocking off the route. State troopers on horseback, shielding the funeral procession from gawkers. A horse-drawn enclosed wagon bearing a simple wooden coffin.

We'd had several conversations with Zach, but he remained adamant about not coming to Charlie's funeral. I continued to ask visitors to pray for him. By Friday afternoon, spent with grief and emotion, we decided to leave town for a few hours. Marie and her children were up at her aunt's home in Lititz. We had not seen our grandchildren since early in the week. We made arrangements to spend the evening with them.

We were making preparations to leave when the phone rang. The voice on the other end was Zach's. "I'm on the train from New York. I should get into Lancaster about 6 p.m. Would you mind sending someone to pick me up?"

Would we mind! Tears and joy intermingled as I took in this miracle. What had changed Zach's mind? As he told us later, pleas from Marie, his niece and nephews, parents, and siblings had softened his heart. But Zach shared that the turning point had been the voice message our Amish friend had left on his answering machine, urging him to forgive his brother and be there to comfort his family.

Zach arrived in time to meet us in Lititz, picked up at the station by his cousin Ben. The children were as delighted as we were to see their uncle. Other family members stopped by. Despite our grief, that evening was such a peaceful, healing respite for all of us as a family.

On Saturday, the sun rose bright and clear, far too beautiful a morning to be burying a son. By this time, I just wanted to get through the day. The funeral was scheduled for 10 a.m. at High View Church of God. This was the church where we'd joyously watched our firstborn and his bride exchange their vows. As we walked in, flowers and music greeted us as they had on that day only a decade earlier. But, oh, what a difference!

My heart broke afresh for Marie and the children, seated in the front row directly in front of the casket, dressed in the black of mourning. My grandchildren wore matching outfits I'd purchased for them that were never worn again. The Welk family sat around Marie. We found our own seats directly across the aisle from them. I took comfort in Josh, Zach, Jon, their wives, my parents, and other family members sitting close around us.

Pastor Dwight Lefever officiated. Grief thickened his voice as he spoke. His dad, Pastor Tom Lefever, had been both Charlie and Marie's pastor since their teen years. Because no public announcement had been made of when and where Charlie's funeral would be held, the attendance was only family and a few friends we'd invited. We discovered afterward that in order to protect the proceedings from a media invasion, Pastor Tom hadn't asked for the usual help from church members. Instead he'd made most of the funeral preparations himself, even purchasing and preparing a soup-and-sandwich luncheon for after the burial. We are so grateful to this day for his kindness to our family.

During the short service, I let my mind go back as Betsy had counseled me, pulling up one precious memory after another of my beloved firstborn son. His wriggling, small body against mine, legs heavy with casts and braces. A little boy running through fields and woods, blue eyes lit up with delight in God's creation. His sweet, shy smile as he showed me some piece of workmanship over which he'd labored. Standing right there where his casket now rested, his face ablaze with love and joy as he looked down into Marie's eyes and uttered the words "I do."

I don't even remember the fifteen-minute drive to the United Methodist Church cemetery in Georgetown, part of Bart Township, walking distance from Charlie and Marie's home. But I remember well my dismay as we approached the little white church. We'd been told the state police would cordon off the funeral procession route and area around the cemetery to permit us to hold the burial service in peace. They had done so, and we'd seen little movement in the countryside during the funeral procession. But as the procession came into view of the church, we could see a horde of news crews and spectators amassed behind the security barrier across the street from the cemetery. Media vans and trucks were parked farther down the street beyond a police barricade.

On either side of the church and cemetery were houses with large trees offering some concealment. Behind the church, just off to the left of the cemetery, were several long storage sheds. But the cemetery itself lay in the open with flat, wide fields stretching all around. As we left the shelter of the funeral convoy, we could see cameras with telescopic lenses immediately shifting toward us.

We were still following my son's casket when another miracle unfolded. It was not a surprise. We'd been alerted the evening before that we could expect it. But that such a thing could even occur was in itself a miracle of forgiveness and grace.

From behind a long, white shed emerged a group of at least thirty black-clad Amish, the men in their tall, wide-brimmed hats, the women in white bonnets. As we reached the grave site next to the pink heart-shaped tombstone of Charlie's own firstborn, Elise Victoria, the group fanned out into a crescent between the grave site and the road, their turned backs offering a solid wall of black to the media cameras beyond the security barricade.

Among the Amish arrivals were both acquaintances and some of the parents of Charlie's victims. Their sober faces under hat and bonnet were so young. All of the parents there were so young. These sweet, grief-stricken families were not of our generation, but that of our children! During the burial service, I saw tears spilling down their faces just as they spilled down my own. Nearby, I saw Marie's pale face and the bewildered sadness in my grandchildren's expressions.

Fresh anger shook me. I'd tried so hard to focus on the good memories. But now I could think only of the terrible wrong Charlie had done. How could these sweet, young parents ever forgive Charlie? How could I ever ask them to? I'd begged my son Zach to forgive his brother. And yet at this moment I was not sure that I as Charlie's mother could ever forgive the unspeakable evil he'd perpetrated on these young parents, his own children, our family.

And yet neither could I stop loving Charlie. He was my son!

I held on to my composure until the brief burial service was finished. Our Amish guests stepped forward one by one to express their condolences. Among the first to approach us were Chris and Rachel Miller, whose two daughters, Lena and Mary Liz, had died in their arms.

Murmuring a greeting to Chuck and me, they added softly, "We are so sorry for your loss!"

Sorry for our loss? I could barely choke out a response. Our son had taken the lives of their two precious daughters. And now here they were comforting us!

It was a moment of sudden, healing clarity for me. Forgiveness is a choice. The Amish spokesman had made it clear. Which meant that it wasn't a feeling. These sweet parents were still as grief-stricken as I was, their hearts broken like mine over the loss of their children. But they had *chosen* to forgive instead of hating, to reach out in compassion instead of anger.

If we cannot forgive, how can we be forgiven? The Amish had said that too. But it was more than that. *I am forgiven! I am not a murderer, but how many wrongs have I done in my life? Yet God has forgiven my sin. He took on human form to pay the penalty on the cross for my sins. How can I in turn not offer the forgiveness I have received—even to my own son? Especially to my own son.*

I did not have to stop *feeling* anger, hurt, and utter bewilderment at the inexplicable, horrific choices Charlie had made. I only had to make a choice. As I had chosen to love my husband. As I had chosen to pursue life instead of death. This time it was a choice to forgive.

And if I did not make that choice? If I did not forgive, I would be left with the same hole in my heart that Charlie had allowed to fill up with bitterness and rage. And look where that had led!

I forgive you, Charlie! I can't say I'm not still angry and confused, because I am. But I choose to forgive you. I love you. I love you so much! I love you as I have since the day I first knew your sweet little body was growing inside mine.

Peace swept over me. And a fresh understanding of just how deep, wide, and high is God's love for me. Because I know just how much I love my son despite his wrong actions. How much more does our heavenly Father love His children, His creation, despite all the wrong choices and actions we make again and again?

I am forgiven! I choose to forgive!

All week I'd been dreading this day. But in the end, our son's funeral proved to be a testimony of the greatest love that anyone could show. In a world that speaks so loudly of rights, the Amish had every right to feel anger, bitterness, and thirst for revenge. Instead, we heard that day only words of kindness and compassion as they greeted Charlie's widow, Marie, his children, our family. The healing we received through their comforting words, the love and caring shown to us from the very beginning, have little precedent in this world of hate and revenge.

My faith and church traditions are very different than those of the Amish. Their ordinances include many practices and beliefs on which we don't see eye to eye. But I have never encountered anyone who has better modeled to me the life and character of Jesus Christ than was displayed to us that day by the Amish of Lancaster County.

What change would we see on this strife-torn planet if everyone in the world came to know and model Amish forgiveness?

14

Facing Firsts

For the Spirit God gave us does not make us timid, but
gives us power, love, and self-discipline.

—2 Timothy 1:7

The next morning I walked into church with some trepidation.
While a number of our church friends had stopped by during the last week to pray with us and offer support, this was
the first time we'd be facing the entire congregation. Would
we encounter the love and compassion we'd received from the
Amish community? Or would we see speculation, condemna-
tion? Surely many must be wondering what we had done or
missed for our son to have committed this crime.

But if so, we did not see or hear such. I fought back fresh tears
as I responded to hugs and murmured sympathy. The worship
music was sweet refreshment to my soul. Pastor Dwight spoke a

few words concerning the events of the last week. Then a rustle of surprise swept across the congregation as my daughter-in-law Marie stood up and walked forward. Her pretty face showed the strain of these last days, but there was courage in her gaze and strength in her voice. She touched briefly on what had happened, then went on to speak of God's grace and healing manifested these last few days in her life, her children, and even the Amish families.

"Please continue to pray for our family," she finished. "And for the Amish families, the first responders, and all who were touched by this tragedy. Rejoice with me too that God *is* working in all our lives through this."

I was so proud of her. Worry for Charlie's wife and children had been an additional burden these last days. But I could lay that burden down. Marie was finding her own healing in this darkness. My sweet daughter-in-law and precious grandchildren were in God's hands. God would use this tragedy and sadness for His good purpose in their lives as well as in mine and others'.

On Monday, I headed back to work and Zach returned home. Just in these few days, we had seen in him such a change in attitude. Before he left, Zach told me, "The world really needs to hear this message of forgiveness. I live every day in a culture that has not seen this."

Little did Zach or I know that over the following years his own piece of this story would become a vehicle to share the message of forgiveness. Little could I have guessed how far God would take me personally in sharing the story.

Many years later, Zach came for a three-week visit. I was scheduled to speak at a church in York, Pennsylvania, and I invited Zach and Chuck to come along with me. It was the first time Zach had ever heard me share my journey to joy through adversity, which included his story as well as Charlie's and my cancer ordeal. After the event, a mother approached me with her teenage daughter, tears streaming down her cheeks.

"I'm embarrassed to call myself a Christian," she cried. "I have forbidden my sister to even come to my funeral. I've actually drawn up a legal document specifying she can't attend. I'm leaving here today to destroy that document and call my sister."

When I asked her what about my story had changed her heart, she responded, "It was Zach's story, hearing how he released his bitterness to forgive and come to his brother's funeral." How that encounter impacted Zach as well as me!

The funeral had been an uplifting experience. But getting back to "normal" life did not always prove easy. Chuck had already returned to work that first Thursday. The encouragement he'd received from his Amish clients, their assurance that they still wanted him to be their friend and in their lives, had been greatly healing to him.

At my own job, colleagues were for the most part kind and welcoming, careful not to bring up recent events in my presence. But a co-worker in my department had been a first responder at the schoolhouse. She was struggling with post-traumatic stress syndrome over all she'd seen, and she could not bear to see me or work near me. She requested reassignment to another department where she wouldn't have to encounter me, and eventually resigned from our place of employment.

Mel Lantz—First Responder, Volunteer EMT

I was driving my delivery truck on Route 741, east of Strasburg, when I heard a radio alert of a mass casualty event at the Nickel Mines schoolhouse. They were requesting five additional ambulances. I couldn't imagine what kind of event could need that many units. I immediately turned my truck around and headed to the scene.

SWAT teams and emergency response had the area cordoned off. I identified myself to the police as an EMT. Walking into the schoolyard, I saw a scene I'll never forget. Such a surge of anger went through me that someone had shot these children. I immediately went into triage mode and began to assess the situation. I could see life-threatening injuries, but I felt so helpless and inadequate, since there were not enough resources at the time to treat the victims.

After the girls were taken care of, I treated an officer with a cut finger. But there was nothing else for me to do. Afterward all the first responders were called to the Bart fire station for a debriefing. How are you supposed to sit there and tell people how you feel when you're not even sure what you're feeling? Eventually I left to finish my deliveries. I wondered why God had me there that day. If that call had come in just five minutes later, I'd have been at this delivery and wouldn't have gotten the call. I had to believe God's hand was in this.

Going home to my children that first night, they just seemed more precious to me. The following days, it felt as though a dark cloud hung over me. I couldn't forget what I'd seen. I remember a phone call from a family member asking about the event and just breaking into tears. My wife encouraged me to go to the viewings for the little girls. We went together. Seeing them at peace, sharing with the families, brought the beginning of healing.

The following Thursday, the schoolhouse was demolished. I took my truck to haul debris. I recognized family members of the victims. One mother asked me how I was doing. I remember thinking, *You just lost your daughter, and you can ask me how I'm doing?* It was like a dagger in my heart, but in a good way.

After "The Happening," as the Amish call the event, I came to know the families well. My wife and I visited the girls who'd survived and their families. I drove a number of times to take one of the survivors to doctor appointments. Sometimes I'd go out with the men for coffee or drive them to the store. That first year was exhausting mentally and physically as I struggled to deal with the trauma. But the connection I developed with the Amish helped both sides in the healing process. My desire was to minister to these families, but I found them ministering to me.

People say forgive and forget. Do I forgive the shooter? Those first moments at the schoolhouse, I was so angry. But I can honestly say I hold no feelings against Charlie or his family. If the families of the victims can forgive, surely I can. I've seen the power of forgiveness, how choosing forgiveness helps and heals people. I will never forget one of the girls' fathers saying, "The journey begins with you making the choice to do that [forgive]."

He wasn't suggesting that forgiving is easy. It's still a process. As to forgetting, I'm not sure I want to forget. If this hadn't happened, I wouldn't have the relationships I have now [with the Amish]. We would never choose this to happen. But it did, and we have to find good in it. These Amish families, and Terri Roberts too, have helped me see this. If you can bring the sides together—those who lost, those who survived—it makes a difference. One thing I've learned is that when you're in grief, if you can reach out to someone else who is also grieving, there is great healing power in this on both sides.

What happens when that exchange occurs? It's God's grace.

Seeing my colleague struggle moved me to pray more deeply for all the EMTs, law enforcement, and other first responders who'd been there that day. I could not blame her, because I too was still struggling. Each new "first" brought tears. The first time I drove past an Amish schoolhouse. Going to the mall and spotting a man's profile that looked like Charlie. Walking into our local hardware store and seeing a young Amish child. Even a hug from Chuck brought a flood of tears that Marie would never again know such an embrace from Charlie.

The tearing down of the Nickel Mines schoolhouse was a mile marker in the healing journey. We concurred completely with the Amish families, who did not want their children to have to walk into that building ever again or to have it become a tourist attraction for the countless outsiders who come every year to explore Amish country. Classes resumed for the surviving children inside the garage of a nearby Amish business while a new school was being built. We were thankful that their teacher, twenty-year-old Emma Mae Zook, was there to welcome them back.

One first I'd been dreading was my first shopping expedition to Costco. I walked through the aisles, steeling myself against whom I might run into, what they would say. Little stands offering food samples are part of the Costco experience. As I paused to pick up a sample, the woman handing them out looked sharply at me and commented, "Hey, I just saw you on TV!"

I froze, my heart plummeting. Then she went on, "I think it was that Sight & Sound commercial. Were you in that?"

Sure enough, not long before I'd participated in the production of a video advertisement for Sight & Sound that was used as a pre-show promotion at the theatre. Quickly regaining my composure, I murmured some response and escaped, only too thankful she had not connected me to recent news.

At our local grocery store, I was not able to avoid recognition. As the checkout employee greeted me, she added, "I am so sorry for what happened. But we do still want you to shop at our store."

"Thank you," I responded, breathing thanks to God for the kindness of the Lancaster County people. "I'm planning on coming again."

In the outside world, things seemed to be very much back to normal. Even the media had largely drifted off to some other new and exciting story. As I drove to work, I saw Amish farmers again in their fields, bringing in the harvest. The fall landscape was as beautiful and serene as it always is in Lancaster County. *How can the world be so normal?* I asked myself. *How can people go about life as though nothing has changed?*

But I realized they were right. The more I focused on those things that were normal, steady, real, the better I was able to get back on track. I found myself returning again and again to the Scripture passage that had meant so much to me going through cancer—Philippians 4:6–7:

> In every situation (*even this unspeakable tragedy!*) . . . with thanksgiving (*Lord, I see even less to give thanks for now than in the cancer, but I will choose to pray with thanksgiving anyway!*), present your requests to God. And the peace of God, which transcends all understanding, will guard your hearts and your minds in Christ Jesus (*oh, yes, heavenly Father, let your peace take hold of my heart and mind, regardless of my feelings!*).

The very next verse, Philippians 4:8, also became significant to me:

> Finally, brothers and sisters, whatever is true, whatever is noble, whatever is right, whatever is pure, whatever is lovely, whatever

is admirable—if anything is excellent or praiseworthy—think about such things (*give me strength, Lord, to focus on the good you have placed in my life, not the evils with which this world abounds!*).

One great help in moving forward was the grief and trauma counseling provided to all involved in this tragedy—our family, the Amish, the first responders, even the area children. Various counselors had come to talk to us from the beginning. A priority was the Bart elementary school that Charlie and Marie's two older children attended. Counselors had been assigned to prepare the teachers to deal with questions and trauma, but also to prepare the other children for my grandchildren's return.

Thankfully, our grandchildren experienced nothing but a compassionate welcome upon their return to classes. A strong factor to which that can be attributed was the counselor assigned to that school, a woman who would have a great and healing impact on my own life. Cheri Lovre was a world-renowned trauma counselor from the Crisis Management Institute in Portland, Oregon. She'd been invited by the school district to bring her grief and trauma expertise into the larger challenge of helping the entire community move toward recovery.

I will never forget my first meeting with Cheri. Chuck was working, so did not attend, but Marie and her parents, Ken and Nadine, were with me. We met with the school administrator, who led us to the library for our meeting with Cheri. Instantly I was set at ease by her warmth and smile. Such a grave circumstance had brought us all together. Yet it was immediately clear that this was Cheri's calling, because her astute questions, the thoughts she had us ponder, not only helped us release our emotions in a healthy way, but offered a safe place to sort through events that remained so unreal and hard to deal with.

We all talked in depth for about two hours. One statement that brought me to fresh tears was made by Ken, Marie's dad. Charlie's father-in-law made a comment suggesting that any father would have been proud to have Charlie Roberts as a son-in-law.

Oh, how it blessed my spirit to hear that from my son's father-in-law! Oh, how I wished Chuck had been there to hear that statement! It was not in any way a mitigation of Charlie's actions. But it was a reminder that there had been another Charlie we all knew and loved.

Cheri spoke as well. I don't remember all she said, but several of her comments are engraved on my mind. Life would never be the same "normal" we'd known, she told us. "You will have to find a new normal."

She also reassured us that our continued grief was to be expected. "You will cry buckets of tears. Right now your buckets are full to overflowing, and nothing has to happen for those tears to flow, but that will gradually subside. It is not that tears will not continue to come. But in time those buckets will no longer be full. Over time, as the level of tears goes down, you'll find more resilience in life, but there will always be an inch of tears in the bottom of that bucket. And that's what will give you a deep capacity for compassion when sharing with others who have faced overwhelming adversity."

Cheri did not stay long in our community. She had to return to her work at CMI in Oregon. But she did not leave our lives. Especially mine. She'd made clear her willingness to be there day or night if I needed to call. My emotions were running high in the weeks that followed, and more than once, I took her up on that offer. Her encouragement and understanding allowed me to move through stages of emotion that at times overwhelmed me.

I count Cheri as one of the most precious gifts God gave me in my healing process. Over the years her wise counsel blossomed into deep friendship. When she came back to the Northeast for various conferences, she always scheduled time to get together for a chat or to visit the Amish families with me. I've visited Cheri in Oregon too. She took time to meet with our son Zach when working in New York City. She was even a part of a documentary program we did for public TV in Canada. I can still pick up the phone at any time of the day or night and be blessed by her gracious counsel.

Cheri Lovre, Trauma Counselor

The Amish hold values that have been true to their communities for generations, and they were founded in a belief that there is something more powerful—and more virtuous—than violence. That they hold these values in our midst—quietly, humbly, but ever present—has a value we can't quite name. Whether it was ever an influence that we would have identified, it became so with the shooting at Nickel Mines.

And so it was that I was told early on, "These people are different. They won't be asking why Charlie did this. They'll see it as God's will." From the first hours of this event, the Amish had gone to Charlie's home to tell his wife and family that Charlie was forgiven. Many times Amish asked what they could do for Marie, Charlie's widow.

So as a community, they live out forgiveness, even now. To greater and lesser degrees, according to the individual, some struggle with forgiveness for a time. But it is their way. What Charles Roberts did that day defies understanding for all of us. We can come up with a story line, an explanation, an answer. But for one, we'll never know what was going on in the tortured heart or soul of this man who was beloved and loving. And even though the Amish live their faith, they are the first to see that having the "English" (all of us who are not Amish) see them as having forgiven Charlie is a burden for some of them. As though somehow now they have to be sure that their children are even more forgiving. More pure. More faithful.

As I met the families on all sides of this event, I found myself relating to one thing. Of all the school shootings to which I'd responded, all the knifings, all the natural disasters, this one was different. In all the school shootings before now, there were many who ran headlong into the wall of anger that was there for any who chose to visit it. The anger of the families can give people a place to join. At Columbine, a faith-based group put fifteen huge crosses in the ground, which means they were putting up crosses representing the deaths of all twelve students, the one teacher, and the two aggressors. The parents of one student who died innocently that day pulled two crosses out of the ground, unable to allow those representing the two boys who did this to be present where their child was represented. The parent in me can entirely identify with that.

When the shooting at Nickel Mines left five little girls dead and five wounded, the Amish didn't react in anger. That isn't to say none of them felt anger. But those who did struggled with it quietly. They didn't teach anger as the way for their children. None put voice to it. Early on, there were those who struggled with whether they individually in their hearts had forgiven Charlie, even though they were grateful that the Amish way is to do so, and that the community as a whole stood in forgiveness, even in the midst of their struggle. That's how we all survive these things. To stand together. To stand with each other. And sometimes to stand *for* each other. And the Amish stand together in support of one another in forgiveness. But the Amish say over and over that if they struggle with this, they must simply pray harder and more diligently. Forgiveness is the way. It is their way. So if they are struggling with forgiveness, they'll simply pray more. Pray earnestly.

What I related to these Amish families was that there had been no other national tragedy at the time—no other event garnering international news—that could have made it possible for the evening news anchors to avoid doing a lead story on forgiveness. They couldn't get pictures of the funerals or the profound grief of the parents or the interviews with adolescents who were seduced by the cameras. They couldn't get pictures of the blood, of the mayhem of the survivors. The network and cable newscasters were left with no choice but to speak of the power of Amish forgiveness and how it mystified most of the rest of us. This to me is a watershed moment in the American conscience and in our national crisis of faith. This to me is the reminder of how God actually meant for us to live—humbly walking every step of our lives in a way that confirms our belief in the goodness of humankind. Rising above the distinctions and differences that divide us and somehow making room for all.

Another amazing blessing in my life was Linda Shoemaker, the guidance counselor at a Strasburg area elementary school. Linda and Cheri actually met that first week at an informal brunch for a few local school counselors who already knew Cheri and her work. The chair of the Pennsylvania School Counselors Association had asked Linda to attend because she had close friends who were Amish. She'd be able to help Cheri understand their culture, needs, and ways. Linda and Cheri were seated next to each other and became good friends. None of us knew at the time that within a few months my grandchildren would be moving into the school district where Linda was counselor. What a peace I felt, knowing my grandchildren were in the care of such a fine woman gifted to meet their needs.

Then there was Kate Zook, whom Marie and I both met through the counseling center (Zook is a common Amish name, and though raised in the culture in her early years, Kate is no longer Amish). She'd been through severe trauma herself as a result of a serious motorcycle accident. She volunteered simply to pray for us and be a friend on call. Over the years, Kate has accompanied both Marie and me on speaking engagements and been there for both of us in countless ways.

I could list so many others. There are not words to express what a tremendous outlet and source of direction it has been to have special friends like these in whom to confide and share the sorrow. I encourage anyone who is going through grief and trauma to seek out at least one person willing to be your listening ear and helping hand, not just short-term, but for the years ahead that it will take to heal completely. And, if at all possible, seek out professional grief or trauma counseling as applicable to your individual situation.

Cheri's words that day in the school library have certainly come true. The tears still come, but the bucket is much smaller these days and needed less often. Those tears that remain have truly given me a more compassionate outlook on this hurting world and the multitudes in it going through adversity every moment of every day.

As to finding a new normal, I learned soon enough what she meant. But I never could have imagined then how interwoven my new normal would be with the very Amish families against whom my son had sinned.

15

Bart Fire Hall

The LORD turn his face toward you and give you peace.

—Numbers 6:26

It was two weeks later when Jake Stoltzfoos, from whom my parents had bought their land, asked Chuck if he could drive their family and a few others to visit the grandparents of Lena and Mary Liz, the seven- and eight-year-old Miller sisters who'd lost their lives. I was invited to come along. Chuck and I recognized that their request for Chuck to be their driver was their way of assuring him, "Roberts, we love you, and we don't hold this against you."

But we were not only asked to drive. They insisted we join them for the visit. Inside the home were gathered at least fifteen visitors, among them a family member who was a volunteer first responder. This was the first time I'd sat and visited in a large group of Amish. I felt both nervous and deeply touched at their warm welcome. The woman sitting next to me asked how I was doing. As I paid my respects to the Miller girls' grandmother (who later joined other grandmothers for a tea in our home), I could see her deep pain, but also an overflowing of forgiveness. We were invited to come again, and there was no mistaking the sincerity of that invitation. Though I neither expected nor really understood their reaction, I was deeply grateful for it. Somehow, it seemed that reaching out to include Chuck and me in their lives offered as much an element of healing to them as it did to us.

Not long afterward, a group of Amish, both men and women, came to visit us at our home. This led to an incident that illustrated the potential pitfalls of two different cultures meeting. The end of our visit had come. As they prepared to leave, I asked if we could pray together first. There were nods of assent. When they stood there silently, I began praying aloud. I didn't realize then that the Amish may recite aloud liturgical prayers, but personal prayer is done only silently. Fortunately, they were gracious about my blunder. Since then I've learned to always ask permission, and if they request I honor their culture, I have always done so.

Then there was Lydia, grandmother of one of the survivors, Sarah Ann Stoltzfus, age eight. Sarah Ann's wounds had left a gaping hole in her skull that looked as though it would need further operations and insertion of a ceramic plate. Oh, how my prayers went up for this sweet child! Though Lydia had no phone in her home, she would seek one out regularly to call me with an update on how Sarah Ann was doing.

I received one such call during a visit to Zach in New York. Zach had offered me and several girlfriends a city tour as a respite from the strain of recent weeks. I was walking down a street in the Soho district of Manhattan when the phone rang. How I rejoiced as Lydia's voice with its unhurried, low-German accent gave me the good news that Sarah's skull wound had closed to the size of a silver dollar and would no longer need a ceramic plate. The wound eventually healed completely on its own.

These interactions were a blessing, because life continued to hold ups and downs. One suggestion Cheri had made was that I should make an effort to watch news coverage of the tragedy at least once. Otherwise I might find myself in an airport or office somewhere and face the sudden, painful shock of seeing my son's face unexpectedly on a screen. It was better to prepare myself in advance.

A short time later, a local TV station ran a special segment on the shooting titled "Five Little Angels." My friend Delores suggested to me, "If you want to see and understand what happened, this is the one you'll want to watch. It is so well done."

I knew my friend and Cheri were right. It was time to take that step. But I also knew it would be heart-searing. I told Chuck about the segment and what Cheri had recommended. But he could not bring himself to watch it.

I asked him, "If I watch, will you sit here and hold my hand?"

He agreed. So I sat at the dining table watching the TV segment while he faced the opposite direction, holding my hand. Our tear buckets overflowed again on that day. One important principle I learned during this time is that we all heal differently. Chuck and I certainly processed our grief in very different ways. To maintain relationships, it is imperative that we respect one another and above all our differences as we allow healing to take place.

An ongoing blessing during all this was the mail that continued to pour in. By now I had a huge basket of cards and letters from people all over the country. While none expressed hostility, some questioned how we could have missed Charlie's mental issues. But most conveyed similar messages: "You are in our prayers. . . . My heart reaches out to another mother's heart. . . . We know you loved your son. . . . This was not the son you knew."

More than a hundred cards came from Amish families. The most precious mail we received was a handmade book that held letters and hand-drawn pictures from family members—adults and children—of the Amish community from across the Strasburg area. The letters showered us with encouragement and love. That book remains one of my most treasured possessions.

Excerpts From Amish Cards

To our unknown friends, Charlie [their name for Chuck] and wife. While our thoughts are with you, we hope you can "keep on keepin' on" as you were! I understand you are a taxi driver, and those are needed. The folks [Amish] will need your friendship as well as you need theirs. . . . Our goal is to help each other "bloom where we are planted" and live one day at a time. That's all we can handle. May God give you strength to meet each new day. Love and prayers.

—John and Lizzie and family

No burden's too heavy, no way is too long, if your hopes are high and your faith is strong!

—Rebecca

Cling to the Lord's Prayer.

—Amish card

Your reaching out to us means more than you'll ever know. . . .
God heals the brokenhearted.

—Amish parents

Yesterday God helped me. Today He did the same. How
long will this continue? Forever. Praise His name.

—Card from unknown Amish writer

Dear friends: Our thoughts and prayers are much with you.
Wishing you strength for each new day. The tears in our
eyes are dried by the hands of a loving Father who under-
stands all our problems, our fears, and despair, when we
take them to Him on the wings of prayer. Wishing you the
peace that passes all understanding.

–Amos and Salomie

"The LORD bless you and keep you; the LORD make his face
shine on you and be gracious to you; the LORD turn his face
toward you and give you peace."

—Quote from Numbers 6:24–26, Amish card

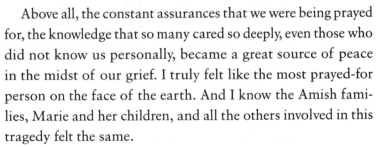

Above all, the constant assurances that we were being prayed
for, the knowledge that so many cared so deeply, even those who
did not know us personally, became a great source of peace
in the midst of our grief. I truly felt like the most prayed-for
person on the face of the earth. And I know the Amish families, Marie and her children, and all the others involved in this
tragedy felt the same.

If anyone wonders whether prayer is an effective use of time,
I can testify that it is. Prayer is where we should be until called
into action. It is where the power is. At times my sorrow was

beyond words. But the awareness of that power lifting me up enabled me to move through the motions into each new day instead of freezing and turning inward to self-pity. To anyone reading this book who was a prayer warrior for us through the days, weeks, and months after our tragedy, thank you from the depths of my heart!

The most formal meeting with the Amish was organized about a month after the schoolhouse tragedy by a local grief counselor, Brad Aldrich, and our own family spokesman, Pastor Dwight Lefever, at the Bart Township fire hall. Bart Township Fire Company was not only the volunteer fire, rescue, and emergency response service for the greater Georgetown area, including Nickel Mines. Its solid redbrick building was also a community center where town meetings, auctions, fund-raising dinners, and much more were hosted. It had been the hub for first responders, media, and families involved throughout the shooting and its aftermath. The families of the victims and the perpetrator, as well as first responders and grief counselors, had been invited to the meeting. Thankfully, media were excluded.

Marie's parents, Ken and Nadine Welk, lived only a few hundred feet from the fire hall. Since we lived a good fifteen minutes' drive from there, we parked at the Welks' home, then walked to the hall with Marie and her parents. As we arrived, the long line of horses and black buggies was an immediate indicator that this was no ordinary community gathering.

Inside, we found the hall filled to overflowing. All of the parents of the victims, as well as many grandparents and other family members, had shown up. Some of the Amish families had even brought their children. There were ten to fifteen grief counselors and a number of first responders. In contrast, our side included Marie, her parents and younger sister, Chuck, and me.

Chuck and I sat next to Amos and Kate Ebersol, who had lost their only daughter, Naomi Rose, age seven. We exchanged glances and nods. I remember looking around the room filled with Amish in black and blue and white. There'd been a time not so long ago when it seemed to me these people who shared my landscape all looked alike. Outside of my own neighbors, I could not tell them apart. Now they were all taking shape as the precious individuals they were.

Pastor Dwight said a prayer. Then one by one, people began to speak. Parents and grandparents poured out their pain. They spoke of not understanding God's ways. But they also spoke of surrender to God's will and forgiveness. They expressed gratitude for all that was being done to provide for the medical and financial needs of the victims. If we as outsiders had been stunned by the Amish display of forgiveness, the Amish themselves seemed just as amazed at the outpouring of love, prayers, and support from "Englishers" all across the continent and even around the world. One unexpected outcome of this tragedy was a new unity and understanding on both sides of two very opposite cultures.

"Today we are all Amish," one Amish spokesman summed up aptly in the aftermath of this tragedy.

Marie spoke. As at the church service that first Sunday, her words conveyed the grace and healing God was working in her life and her children, as well as thankfulness to the Amish community for their love and support. Despite her own tragedy—or perhaps because of it—we were seeing our daughter-in-law's faith and spiritual maturity growing by leaps and bounds.

Then I had my own opportunity to speak. I quoted Philippians 4:6–7, the Scripture passage that had come to mean so much to me going through cancer, and Philippians 4:8, which was giving me strength to move forward. I shared how God had used these verses to teach me to give thanks, whatever the circumstance. I shared how God's peace was guarding my heart and mind afresh in this new storm season of my life, though Satan would like to plant seeds of doubt, deceit, and despair. I shared how I was learning to focus on good things and not evil.

During the meeting, I don't think the tears stopped flowing all around the room. As I was speaking, Amos and Kate were signifying with nods and looks their support for my words. As they shared their grief, I wept with them. By the end, all of us had spilled out so much pain, so many tears. But there had also been so much comfort, compassion, and healing.

After the meeting broke up, I saw a number of the young Amish women gathering together to talk. At that time, I didn't know which were the mothers of victims or survivors and which were extended family. In time, I would come to know each of them intimately. But I remember Mary Liz, the mother of six-year-old Rosanna King. Rosanna's injuries had been the worst of the survivors. Her brain was so damaged that she could not communicate, walk, or eat. Her medical team had let the parents know there was nothing further they could do, and the family had taken her home, understanding that she would likely pass into eternity within a few days or weeks. But Rosanna was still tenaciously holding on to life.

"We don't know if God will heal Rosanna. Maybe what He wants for her is that the memory of everything that happened to her be gone," I overheard Mary Liz telling another young mother. She also mentioned that perhaps God wanted Rosanna to be a reminder of that day.

Her young, vibrant mother's spirit wrenched my heart. Just looking at the group of Amish women took me back to my own early Bible study days when all of us young mothers would huddle together to chat about our families. *This isn't the way life should have been!* I wailed inwardly. But I had to accept that *It is the way it is! And with their youth and such strength, they* will *move forward—just like Marie has.*

The meeting ended with a distribution of groceries, gifts, and more cards that had been collected for the Amish families as well as for Marie and her children. One very special gift was a wooden doll bed an Amish family had handcrafted for our granddaughter. That they had thought of Charlie's young daughter left fatherless in all this was just one more display of Amish love and forgiveness.

As we "Englishers" walked back to the Welks', we watched as everyone else left in their buggies. For all of the pain, the tears, the emotion shared, it had been a time of deep healing. I think everyone there that day would agree with me that we were returning home with our hearts lighter than when we'd come.

Shortly after the meeting at the fire hall, Cheri Lovre graciously volunteered to accompany me on a visit to the home of Christ (pronounced like the first half of Christian) and Mary Liz King, parents of six-year-old Rosanna, who alone among the survivors remained in critical condition. Her young parents lived in the constant limbo of neither being able to grieve and move on nor welcome their daughter back to normal life. I didn't know if I could contain my emotion, so I was deeply grateful for Cheri's presence. If I couldn't find the right words, she would.

This was a Sunday afternoon. In the Amish tradition, church services are held every other Sunday in various homes on a rotating basis. The Sundays in between are set aside for visiting, and as we drove onto the King property, we could see a number of buggies filling the yard. My stomach immediately tensed. I had not prepared myself to face an entire group, but was eased by the realization that at least I wouldn't be alone with the King family.

The King family had two boys at that time, including Rosanna's older brother Leroy, who had been among the group of boys who'd run for help when they'd been forced out of the schoolhouse. As Cheri and I pulled up, the boys ran out to meet us.

"Are you here to visit Rosanna?" Leroy asked excitedly. He added with a big smile, "My mom says you are welcome. Come on in."

The boys directed us where to park our vehicle. They were so open and friendly, I soon relaxed. When we entered the house, we found that chairs had been set up in a large circle around the living room in preparation for visitors. Rosanna was there in a wheelchair. Cheri and I were immediately ushered over to sit right next to her. At six years old, she was such a beautiful little girl, so sweet and serene, though she could not speak, and it was difficult to tell how much she was taking in.

In time Rosanna would become an important part of my life. But at that moment, all I could take in was how this cherished child's life had been turned upside down by my son. After a while some visitors would leave. New visitors would come in, walk around the circle shaking each person's hand, including ours, and then sit to chat awhile. I smiled and spoke to Rosanna and chatted with her mother, Mary Liz. I don't remember what I said, but I managed to hold myself in check until Cheri and I were back in our vehicle.

Then I dissolved into tears and cried and cried. Rosanna was only six years old. She'd had a whole life ahead of her. Now that life had been snatched away, and the road ahead was such a rocky one for this precious child and her family. How could this be?

The faith of Rosanna's parents that their daughter was in God's hands, that God had His own very special plan for her life, was a comfort to which I clung. *God, you can bring beauty from ashes, you can bring good from evil. Let it be so in this child's life!*

16

A New Normal

The LORD has . . . sent me to bind up the brokenhearted,
to proclaim freedom for the captives . . . to comfort all
who mourn . . . to bestow on them a crown of beauty
instead of ashes.

—Isaiah 61:1–3

In January, I made the decision to visit each of the Amish families with children in the Nickel Mines schoolhouse. The connections formed during that meeting in Bart fire hall had stirred something in my heart. The gathering had been healing. But it was not enough. I felt that I needed to reach out personally to these families affected by our son's actions. The warm welcome we'd received to this point encouraged me. There was no fear of rejection or anger.

By now, three months after the events at Nickel Mines schoolhouse, life had indeed returned largely to a new normal. We'd survived more "firsts." Charlie's birthday and wedding anniversary. Our first Thanksgiving without Charlie. Our first Christmas.

For Christmas, we'd chosen to leave Lancaster County altogether. Every moment, every scene of the holiday season in Lancaster was fraught with memories. For the children, above all, we decided it was important to make new memories as a family that held nothing of the past. So we took the money I'd been saving the last few years for the sun-room and booked a Disney Christmas cruise. A kind donor provided cruise tickets for Marie and her children. The sun-room funds provided tickets for Chuck and me, my parents, Jon and Megan, Josh and Keturah, as well as Josh's daughter, Maddi.

The cruise proved to be all we'd hoped. Included was a stopover at Disney's own Caribbean island. Sand instead of snow, warm breezes, blue-green surf, palm trees, and seafood were not just a distraction, but added up to so many new fun-filled memories. I could see the burdens rolling off Marie's shoulders while the children's excited squeals and laughter were not only evidence they were enjoying themselves, but music to a grandmother's ears.

We were especially grateful for those good memories because shortly after our return, Marie and the children went through another loss. Dale, Charlie's yellow Labrador, had somehow escaped the yard and been hit by a car. We went over that evening to spend time with Marie and the children. There we witnessed once again God's grace in the midst of loss. That very day a total stranger had sent our grandchildren a gift basket. Along with cookies and a note were three adorable stuffed puppies. They'd arrived just in time to give comfort to the children as Marie shared the bad news.

For us too, it was a painful loss. We'd loved Dale. But even more, he'd been Charlie's dog, another part of our son now gone.

Meanwhile, I was making preparations for my plan to visit the Amish schoolhouse families. One ostensible reason for the visits was to deliver a book Cheri Lovre had written on healing. Cheri has written several books and countless other resources in the area of crisis management and dealing with trauma. But she'd produced this book specifically for these Amish families, its text and illustrations designed for their cultural background. She'd sent me a printed copy for each family we'd be visiting.

I had by now contacted three of the families and set up appointments to visit. I talked over my plans with Chuck. He did not share my need to do this or feel that he could handle the personal interactions. It was a fresh reminder that we were coming to this situation as very different people. Being sensitive to each other and where we are in our healing process takes patience, insight, and a willingness to accept each other where we are.

If I still had much to learn in this area, by now I'd recognized that I needed to let Chuck heal in his own way and at his own pace. So I didn't push him any further on the subject. Instead, I called my new friend Kate Zook, who'd so kindly urged me to contact her for any need I might have.

Kate immediately volunteered to accompany me. She also encouraged me to buy a children's game for each family that could help function as an icebreaker. So, walking through toy aisles, I searched for games that would be appropriate to the Amish culture as well as the differing ages of the children. So many of the games our own children had played, like Monopoly or Life, were centered on goals and activities alien to the Amish. Among the games I finally settled on were Jenga, a tower-building game that uses wooden blocks, and Mancala, a game that uses beads.

I'd scheduled two visits for that first day. The first was to the farm of Chris and Rachel Miller, who had lost two daughters,

Lena and Mary Liz. As Kate and I drove up their farm lane, we saw several buildings. Amish farms typically have a main house and a smaller "dawdi house," to which the parents will eventually move once their children are grown, leaving the main house to an older son and his family. Other siblings may build houses on the family property as well. Looking around, I realized we hadn't checked as to which was Chris and Rachel's home.

Eventually we discovered they were living in the main house. Since we were only two visitors, we were not ushered into the formal parlor, but the kitchen, which is the center of any Amish home. The Millers had three surviving children, two boys and a girl. They were still young enough that they spoke little English, which Amish children typically learn once they start school. But Kate spoke Pennsylvania Dutch, so she translated for me while I let the children pick out a game.

It was evident this young couple was still grieving, but they welcomed us warmly, thanking us for the book and game we'd brought. We chatted easily around a large wooden table. Rachel mentioned that they had been married the same month and year as our Charlie and Marie. There were none of the modern appliances that lightened my own housework. But the simple farm kitchen was sparkling clean and radiated peace and calm.

I shared that next we'd be visiting Crist and Lizzie Stoltzfus, who had two daughters in the schoolhouse—twelve-year-old Anna Mae, who had died, and eight-year-old Sarah Ann, who was recovering from her injuries. Chris asked how Chuck was doing and why he hadn't joined me in this visit. I explained Chuck's hesitation about facing the families and knowing what to say to them.

Chris responded with an understanding chuckle. "Well, you won't have to worry about that with Crist Stoltzfus. He'll carry the conversation just fine! Chuck won't need to be concerned."

When Kate and I left the Millers, we stopped by my house. I looked over at Kate. "Do you mind waiting in the car while I talk to Chuck?"

She nodded, and I went inside. I told Chuck what Chris Miller had shared. He consented to go with me. Kate left us then, and Chuck and I drove to the Stoltzfus home. Here we found a very different scene: a room filled with numerous family members—too many to recall exactly—and a house filled with warmth and activity. A traveling chiropractor was there with an adjustment bench. This homeopathic avenue of medical treatment is very popular among the Amish. Grandpa was on the bench, being worked on. The Stoltzfuses have a big family, and numerous children sat around a dining table playing a board game while the rest were in a semicircle of chairs.

We'd been expected, so chairs had been set out all around the living room. Crist and Lizzie Stoltzfus, Grandma, and other family members were already gathered there awaiting us. Grandma was rocking the youngest Stoltzfus sibling, a baby only a few months old.

Crist Stoltzfus greeted us with a genuine smile and warm, firm handshake. As we'd been told, he definitely displayed a kind, inviting personality. I don't know if Chris Miller had given him an advance warning, but he did not let the conversation lag once. He introduced us to each of the gathered family members.

By then I'd spotted eight-year-old Sarah Ann at one end of the dining table. She was working on homework with a neighbor who was tutoring her to catch up on the schooling she'd lost during her recovery. Sarah Ann glanced up at us with a shy look, then immediately looked back down. I knew she recognized us as the parents of the man who'd hurt her, and I didn't want to make her uncomfortable, so I remained at a distance while I let the children pick out a game.

After a few moments, Grandma surrendered the baby and took her turn on the chiropractic bench. I visited with Lizzie and the others while Crist pulled Chuck into conversation. To my relief, Chuck seemed completely at ease, talking comfortably with Crist Stoltzfus about the local market and other interests in common. Crist knew some of the standholders at the market with whom Chuck interacted.

As with earlier visits, this Amish family showed us warmth and kindness, but their pain was also evident. They didn't minimize their grief at losing one daughter and dealing with the severe injuries of the other. Crist spoke openly of losing work because of spending so much time at the hospital. We were comforted to hear that the Nickel Mines Foundation had received enough donations that no family had to face financial burdens on top of everything else.

During all of this, from the corner of my eye, I could see that Sarah Ann was absorbing our conversation. When we rose to leave, her father went over to her and encouraged her to come and greet us. I could sense her reluctance, and she clung close to her father as she came forward. But she greeted us obediently, giving us a polite smile.

What a precious day that was. In my memory I can still feel the inviting warmth of Crist Stoltzfus's gestures, see Lizzie nodding and smiling, and the sweet, timid look on Sarah Ann's face. And to see my husband interacting freely with them—wow! Eight years later when I drop in to visit, I am eagerly greeted by Sarah Ann with a very welcoming, warm smile.

From that day forward, Chuck went with me for each of the family visits. They were not all so easy. We visited John Fisher, father of thirteen-year-old Marian, who'd so bravely asked to be shot first, as well as eleven-year-old Barbie, who was still recovering from shoulder injuries, and nine-year-old

Emma, who'd escaped. John was a dairy farmer from whose farm Charlie had collected milk. The family had known Charlie. Charlie had known their children. They were more outspoken about all that had happened. How could Charlie have done this to children he knew? To a family who had trusted him and treated him with nothing but respect? We had no more answers than they, but could only share their pain and bewilderment.

Amos and Kate Ebersol, who had sat next to us in the fire hall, lived at that time in a small house with four young sons. Seven-year-old Naomi Rose had been their only daughter. The new Amish schoolhouse was being built on a donated lot within a stone's throw of their home. When we visited them, concrete had just been poured for the school foundation. As we arrived, Amos quietly and Kate warmly welcomed us. The four boys observed us from a distance, though they were attentive to our conversation.

Then a half-grown Jack Russell terrier, a recent birthday gift for Naomi Rose, dashed past us into the house. The puppy had managed to walk through the fresh concrete. In chasing down the terrier and cleaning up the mess its paws had left, the ice was broken. Our visit that day became the first in what has become over the years a very special friendship. Chuck and I both have had the privilege of traveling and speaking with Amos and Kate in the after-years. But more on that later.

Our visit to Daniel and Annie Stoltzfus, parents of Rachel Ann, encouraged me in an entirely different way, which I'll share about later.

I was glad that Cheri and I had an opportunity to visit earlier before Chuck and I entered the King home, which was the most difficult visit of all. Rosanna's family was very gracious and we chatted a while. Rosanna was brought out to the living room in her wheelchair to visit with us. I recall a comment made by

Rosanna's dad, Christ, alluding to the fact that they were glad that the perpetrator wasn't someone off the street, but that Charlie had come from a good, stable Christian home. This brought comfort to my husband and me.

These visits forged a bond between us that I will always cherish. It is a unity I would not have thought possible given our vastly different cultures. These growing relationships will last a lifetime. All things are possible with God!

I recently pulled into the Millers' driveway for a visit to greet the newest addition to their family. Susan, a toddler at the time her sisters were snatched away, greeted me with the broadest smile and the warmest welcome. It touched my heart beyond any imagination. What could have been bleak and dark has turned into a fountain of blessing. These relationships were born out of a sinful act, but as a result of submission and obedience to God, He has made something new to be treasured.

A prayer for each of us should be, *Take every part of me and bring healing if it glorifies you and furthers your kingdom.*

17

Peace Child

I [Jesus] have told you these things, so that in me you may
have peace. In this world you will have trouble. But take
heart! I have overcome the world.

—John 16:33

In February 2007, I received an unexpected invitation, the ripples
of which continue to impact my life. My mother's friend Ruth
Powers is the mother of Chuck Powers, who with his wife,
Cathy, are the missionary friends whose ministry I had visited in
Toulouse, France. My mother and Ruth met through those early
homeschool experiences when the Powerses helped homeschool
Charlie, and they have remained friends ever since.

For years Ruth had been part of an outreach that hosts exchange students from Japan. Even in Japan, the news of the
Amish schoolhouse shooting and the story of Amish forgiveness

had made the rounds of TV and radio. This semester's group of Japanese exchange students had prepared a gift for the surviving Amish schoolchildren. Ruth called my mother to ask if she'd like to go along to deliver the gift. I was invited as well.

At first I was hesitant. The new schoolhouse was not yet finished, so the remaining students—or scholars, as the Amish term their school-age children—were still meeting in the garage that had been their temporary classroom since a week after the shooting. How would these children feel about me, the mother of their assailant, attending such an event? But Ruth and my mother encouraged me to go. At last I agreed to go along as a "fly on the wall" to observe.

The gift the Japanese students had prepared was a mobile made up of one thousand origami cranes folded from paper in every color of the rainbow. These long-necked, long-legged birds, most commonly white with black-edged wings, hold a very special meaning in Japanese culture. A Japanese legend says that a person who makes a thousand origami cranes will have a wish granted by a crane, which the ancient Japanese believed lived one thousand years. Mobiles with a thousand cranes were given as gifts to newborn babies or by fathers to a son or daughter on their wedding day to bring good fortune.

After the world's first atomic bombs wiped out Hiroshima and Nagasaki, Japan, killing or injuring more than two hundred thousand Japanese, and bringing to an end World War II, the thousand origami cranes gained new significance. A young girl named Sadako Sasaki was only two years old when she survived the Hiroshima bombings, but she later developed leukemia from the radiation poisoning. During her illness, she began saving her medicine wrappers and folding them into origami cranes. Her wish upon reaching a thousand cranes was to be healed and to see a world at peace without nuclear war. She completed one thousand cranes just before her death at age twelve. While her wish for a world at peace has never been realized, neither has the world seen another nuclear attack.

Sadako became known as the "peace child." Today her statue holding high a crane with outstretched wings forms part of the Children's Peace Monument, located in Hiroshima Peace Memorial Park, which commemorates the thousands of child victims of the bombings. Origami cranes are offered daily at the memorial as a remembrance and a wish for world peace. Giving one thousand origami cranes to those who have endured hardship is now in the Japanese culture a symbol of solidarity in their suffering. These Japanese students had created this mobile for the Amish schoolhouse children and wanted to share it with them personally.

There were eight to ten Japanese students, enough to fill a large van. When we arrived at the temporary school, what immediately stood out to me was how unbalanced the Amish class seemed. There were eleven boys, but only four girls—Emma, who had escaped, and three of the survivors who were now recovered enough to return to school: Sarah Ann, Rachel Ann, and Esther. Barbie was still undergoing surgeries, while Rosanna would never be able to return to school except to join in with celebrations and special occasions with her brothers and classmates. The stark reality of why there were so many boys compared to girls wrenched my heart.

Their teacher, Emma Mae, was only twenty years old, and like her scholars seemed so young to have undergone the trauma of recent months. But she greeted us with quiet aplomb and displayed the grace and competence of a teacher twice her age. As Ruth Powers explained the purpose for the group's visit, my instinct was to shrink into a corner and hide behind the Japanese students. But then Ruth announced that we were all going to introduce ourselves. Somehow I found myself thrust forward. I introduced myself and mentioned that I was the mother of Charlie Roberts. It was clear the children already knew exactly who I was, but the glances my way were not unfriendly.

After the Japanese students presented their gift and the mobile was hung from the ceiling at the front of the class, the Japanese students brought out paper and showed the Amish scholars how to fold their own origami cranes. Since the Japanese students spoke little English, I joined them going from desk to desk to help the children understand how to fold their cranes. Sitting in the last desk of the last row was a little blond-haired, blue-eyed boy. As I bent down to help him, he looked up at me with a big smile.

"I heard you are visiting all the families," he said. "Are you coming to visit us?"

How deeply that touched my heart. This little boy knew exactly who I was. My son's actions were the reason his schoolroom held three boys for every girl. But like the adults of his community, rather than reacting in anger, he wanted to welcome me to his home!

I held my composure until we left the classroom. Then I admit I burst into tears. The Japanese students surrounded me and comforted me. That day was just the beginning of what I call my "Japanese connection."

Shortly after this, Chuck and I finished our round of family visits. But these visits were not the last expression of Amish grace we experienced. Spring was now approaching, a return of life to the frozen ground of Lancaster County. The new schoolhouse was finished. Funds from the Nickel Mines Accountability Committee Foundation provided for the reconstruction. In April, the children moved to the new building, now renamed

New Hope School. Several girls transferred from other Amish schools to help restore the class gender balance.

The slowly warming earth, the green grass sprouting around the new schoolhouse, the budding leaves and flowers were the outward expression of new life and fresh beginnings in our own family as well as the Amish. The first baby was born, a daughter, to schoolteacher Emma's sister-in-law, who'd been visiting the schoolhouse on October 2. Her parents named her Naomi Rose. Other mothers in the group were pregnant or had new babies. Another baby girl was named Rosanna.

In my own life, spring was heralded by the noise of hammer and saw, the screeching of dragged boards and the thud of rafters dropped into place. My sun-room was rising at last in the backyard. This fulfillment of a dream was even more special because it had come about through a completely undeserved, certainly unexpected gift of Amish love.

This joyous miracle began to unfold not long after Charlie's funeral. Chuck had begun driving again for the Amish builder whose phone call to our son Zach had brought about such a change of heart. Chuck also drove for one of his partners. Theirs was the construction firm we'd originally consulted for a price estimate to build the sun-room. The two men asked Chuck how plans were coming along.

By then we'd already designated those funds for our Christmas cruise to make new memories as a family. So when Chuck passed their query on to me, I responded, "Well, we sure won't have funds to build until we can save again. Just let them know we'll call back in a couple of years."

Chuck told them, and their immediate response was "With all she has gone through, your wife needs her sun-room now."

The two men came over and began laying out plans. Our original design had been a sixteen-by-sixteen-foot room. One brought up the health meetings I was hoping to conduct in the sun-room. "Are you sure that will be big enough?"

"Well, it would be nice to have it bigger," I admitted, "but I'm sure we can make do with sixteen by sixteen."

"No, you need more room," he insisted. "We'll make it sixteen by twenty."

Our Amish friend, his partners, and their construction team broke ground in early May. We bought windows, and my son Josh pitched in with the trim work and painting. But the Amish builders insisted on providing materials, labor, and much more. The blessing of coming down each morning to watch the dawn's light play over each new stage of construction lifted my heart, transforming sorrow into joy. By the end of July, it was finished enough to become the new heart of our home.

The room itself is more windows than walls. Indoors it is painted sunshine yellow with white trim. At the far end, with its glass peak, is a panoramic view of farmland and the valley with the tree line, where Charlie spent so much time as an adventurous teen. French doors open onto a patio on the side. Best of all, just as I'd always dreamed, the bank of large windows on both sides offers the rising sun to the east and the vivid sunsets to the west and keeps the room filled with light from dawn to nightfall.

The windows are made of a special refracting glass that blocks harmful UV radiation, so I don't need to ration my enjoyment of this gift. A pair of sofas appropriated from elsewhere in the house and ample lounging cushions offer comfortable seating. But my own favorite spot is a window seat my son Josh built for me in a back corner of the sun-room. In the morning I sit there with my Bible and a cup of tea, watching the sun rise over the valley. In the evening I curl up to watch the sunset's gorgeous hues pale from red and orange to green and dark blue above the wooded ridge.

In good weather, I open the windows and enjoy a soft breeze on my face, the song of birds, the rattle of my Amish neighbor Chris's horse-drawn mower cutting alfalfa. When storms come, a glassed-in peak on the north side allows me to watch the roiling thunderheads and flashes of lightning, enjoying God's handiwork from a place of complete shelter and safety. When the snow falls, I turn on the spotlight outside and the gas fireplace stove at the left front corner, and relish the warmth of the room and my cup of tea.

As I'd hoped, it has also become a gathering place for family and friends alike, where I host teas and other events with the Amish, and my health meetings. And even more than I envisioned, it has become my own personal sanctuary.

In all the years since, a day has not gone by that I do not thank God for my sun-room—and for the compassion and kindness God laid on the hearts of the men whose own community had been hurt so badly to fulfill a desire of my heart. To me, it is not only a gift of love from the Amish, but from heaven itself.

Another memorized Scripture comes to mind as I sit curled up in my window seat, looking out on a drizzly dawn, mist lying in white pools across the fields. It is Psalm 46:10: "Be still, and know that I am God."

There is a reason my sun-room brings to mind that verse. Outside its walls, the sun may shine brightly to the music of birdsong and soft breezes whispering through the trees. Or storms may lash torrents of water across the glass to the crash of lightning and roar of thunder. But within its sturdy shelter, I find only stillness, tranquility, and peace.

And so with the circumstances of my life. The years bring seasons of tranquil sunshine and seasons of renewed tempest. I can take for granted the sunshine and fret over the storms. Instead I am called to be still and trust my well-being to the sheltering hand and loving providence of my heavenly Father. No drop of rain or gust of wind can touch me except by His permission. I sit here now, alone but never alone, listening for His still, small voice, waiting for Him to speak. As my heart grows quiet like the room around me, I feel His presence. And in that presence, I find peace, healing, renewal, even joy.

If my sun-room has been a greater blessing than I ever envisioned, my prayer from the beginning has been that it would be used to bless others also. So I extend a welcome to come join me here. May others find healing and comfort within these walls of glass that look out upon God's beautiful creation. May the peace of God always be present in the serenity of this place, and may His amazing grace and love fall upon all who enter.

18

Moving Forward

The sovereign LORD is my strength; he makes my feet
like the feet of a deer, he enables me to go on the heights.
—Habakkuk 3:19

If I sought out the sanctuary of my sun-room, this was in part
because other changes that spring had brought proved far more
difficult for me to handle. Above all, our daughter-in-law Marie's wedding. In time I would come to love and appreciate and
thank God for the introduction of a man named Dan into the
lives of our grandchildren and our son's widow. But I can con-
fess now that in the beginning I did not handle matters so well.

A few weeks after Charlie's death, Marie had shared with us
her reconnection with a distant family friend whom she had not
seen since she was a child. We'd heard nothing but good about
Dan. He was reputed to be a godly man, with two children of his

own, a son the same age as Marie's daughter and a daughter a few years older. We'd heard from our grandchildren of playdates with Dan's kids and were glad they were making new friends.

Not long after that, Marie and her children had traveled to Toulouse, France, to spend three weeks with my nephew Ben Hildebrand and his wife, Michelle, who had always been close friends of Marie and Charlie, as well as Michelle's parents, Chuck and Cathy Powers. We left shortly after their return for our family Christmas cruise.

In early January, Marie shared with us that she and Dan had agreed to begin formally dating. I was stunned at my own visceral reaction. My daughter-in-law was young and lovely. I knew there would be loneliness after Charlie's death. I had expected God would eventually bring a new husband to share her life, provide a new father for my fatherless grandchildren. Marie tells the beautiful love story of how God brought her and Dan together in her own book, *One Light Still Shines*.[1] There was no mistaking this was God's leading.

But not so soon! my heart cried. I was not ready to see my son's widow with another man. And what about our grandchildren? Marie had been wonderful since Charlie's death at keeping us involved in her family's life. We'd babysat our grandkids, participated in family events, taken our grandson to soccer games. What would it mean for our relationship with them if they became part of a new family?

I did not even want to meet this new man in her life. At the same time, I knew the problem was my heart, not Marie's decision. I remember well a day in mid-January when we'd invited Marie and the kids over for dinner. She asked if she could bring Dan along to introduce him to us. I said no. I didn't feel I could

1. Marie Monville, *One Light Still Shines* (Grand Rapids, MI: Zondervan, 2013).

handle it. Oh, how I regretted my decision later. Marie was gracious about it, but I knew she'd found my decision hurtful.

But at the beginning of February, Marie was hosting a Super Bowl party. I knew Dan would be there and decided it would be a good time to meet him. If I found my emotions overwhelming, I'd be able to leave, as I wouldn't have been able to do in my own home. I will never forget Dan walking toward me as we entered. He is a tall man, calm and outgoing. I felt my misgivings ease.

A week or so later, Marie brought Dan's son to church with her own children. The church met at that time in the Lancaster Mennonite High School cafeteria. Instead of pews, we sat around tables. I was seated at one table when I saw Dan's son sitting with my grandchildren at a nearby table. This sweet little blond boy could soon be part of our family, I realized. I prayed for God to help me accept this new change in our lives, to accept both this child and his father. Then I knelt down beside the table where they were sitting and forced my mouth into a smile.

"I'm Gran," I said.

We had a delightful conversation. I remember vividly telling myself, *This child is so cool. This dad can't be all bad!* Later I met his sister and found these kids to be delightful. Maybe this was going to work!

On Valentine's Day, Dan proposed and Marie accepted. Over the following weeks, I saw more of Dan as the two began planning their wedding. As I saw Marie's happiness and excitement and the joy of the children with their new brother and sister, the evident love of Dan toward both Marie and her children, my heart softened.

About this time another visit to an Amish family particularly spoke to my heart. Chuck and I went to the home of Daniel and Annie Stoltzfus, the parents of eight-year-old Rachel Ann, who had been injured in the shooting. They asked how Marie and the children were doing. I shared that God had provided the man who would become Marie's husband and daddy to my grandchildren. My emotion was evident, and Daniel asked if he could tell us a story.

He shared that his mom and Annie's dad had passed away within a short period of time. Within a year the remaining spouses had decided to marry each other. Some of the siblings on either side wondered if it was a good idea. But that was three years earlier, and they were happily married.

The warm smile on Daniel's face as he told the story provided reassuring relief and an avenue for my husband and me to see things differently. His words spoke encouragement into our lives to become accepting and understanding of how God was working in Charlie's family.

Marie had wanted to move from the house where she and Charlie had lived to make a new beginning elsewhere for both her and the children. She and Dan decided on a new home for both families to begin their joint life together. It was not very many miles away, but far enough to put our grandchildren in a new school district where their identity would not be the "children of the Amish schoolhouse shooter" or Marie constantly identified as his wife.

The house itself was a beautiful "stick home," as Charlie would have called it, erected on a site that was a far cry from the small home in which Charlie and Marie had lived. Marie and her children moved there in April. Dan and his family would move in after the wedding. It was wonderful to visit and see the excitement of our grandchildren in their new home. But the first time I walked through the house, my heart was heavy because I knew how much my son with his gifts for building and carpentry would have loved it.

But I could not let my grief tarnish the new happiness of my grandchildren and their mother. I "oohed" and "ahhed" appropriately, though I will admit to tears once I was alone. We have choices to make in life. We can choose to look for the good and celebrate the joy of others, or we can concentrate on our own emotions. I made a deliberate choice that day to look outside my own understanding and seek what God's will was in this situation. And it became increasingly apparent that Marie and Dan's union was indeed God's doing and God's blessing.

The wedding was scheduled for May 25, 2007, though the final details and exact location were held in reserve until the last hours to avoid a media invasion. Two days before the wedding, our phone rang. When I picked it up, Marie was on the line. "Do you think Dad [as she called Chuck] would be willing to walk me down the aisle with my dad?"

It was a wonderful gesture. I responded, "Wow! I don't know, but you can sure ask him."

She did, and Chuck was honored to say yes. As he and Ken walked Marie down the aisle, I joined the other moms up front. My other sons and their wives were all present to offer their encouragement and support. Marie was once again a beautiful bride. Our three grandchildren and Dan's two children made up their bridal party. A special moment came when all seven lifted candles from the altar and together as one family lit the unity candle in the center. For me, it was inevitable that my thoughts flew back to an earlier wedding, but the joy of that day far outweighed any tears. I could wholeheartedly give thanks for what and how God had provided for Marie and her children.

Healing is not a steady upward slope, but rather an up-and-down undulation that more resembles a roller coaster. Only three weeks later, we faced one more "first" since Charlie's death—Father's Day. My heart was already heavy as Chuck and I left our car to walk into the church. Marie, Dan, and the children had arrived ahead of us. Just as I entered the church, I saw my six-year-old grandson running past me.

"Daddy!" he called.

I realized my grandson was calling out to Dan. It was like a hot knife through a stick of butter. Searing pain gripped my heart. I turned around and walked back outside. I felt God saying to me, "Find something to be thankful for!" The verse I'd clung to all these months came to mind: "In everything *with thanksgiving* present your requests to God."

How can I give thanks? I cried out inwardly. *It should be Charlie my grandson is running to this day. What is there to give thanks for in this circumstance?*

Then it hit me like a slap in the face. How could I even voice such a thought? God had given me exactly what I'd prayed for. *What can I be thankful for? I can be thankful that my grandchildren have a wonderful, godly man to call Daddy on this Father's Day!*

In that moment God gave me the grace to reenter the church with peace in my heart, hug my grandchildren, and greet with a smile my new step-son-in-law. Since that day I have never ceased to give thanks for the man God brought into our lives to father my grandchildren and bring joy and love to their mother.

That is not to say that even today there are not difficult thoughts of how life might have been. However, I will not allow myself to dwell there. As Cheri Lovre once told me, some tears will always remain at the bottom of the bucket, but they can serve as a reminder of the days that were good and memorable.

By July I felt I'd learned that lesson well. Life was back on an even keel. Our "new normal" of Amish friendships had brought great joy to our lives. Marie and her children were provided for. However painful these past months had been, I had indeed seen

God bring light out of darkness, good from evil. It was time I put this season of my life behind me and move forward.

So I was a little taken aback when a co-worker at Sight & Sound Theatre asked if I'd like to share my story with a group of Japanese exchange students their church was sponsoring. I was no public speaker. I'd grown comfortable sharing my cancer story in a small-group setting. But standing on a platform was something far more intimidating. The trauma of these last months seemed far too intimate to share. Besides, how could a middle-aged woman like me connect with Japanese teenagers?

I went home, talked to Chuck, prayed about it. The more I prayed, the more convicted I felt that this was something I needed to do. I accepted the invitation and then began to ponder how I could relate my life story to students from another culture on the far side of the planet. I was awakened in the middle of the night by thunder crashing and lightning flashing. I descended the stairs to my glass-enclosed sun-room.

As I watched the wet night sky, it occurred to me that storms were one thing with which everyone could identify. In my own country, Hurricane Katrina was still fresh in everyone's memory. Not long before, the worst tsunami in recorded history had ravaged many parts of Asia. Japan, above all, was a country that knew well the devastation of typhoons and tsunamis, storms that could totally uproot and change the course of one's life.

So I prepared to share about my own life storms. The gentle ones that brought moisture to water the land. The hurricane of cancer that I'd once believed to be a storm that could never be surpassed. And then the tsunami of Charlie's actions that had altered my life forever. But more than the storms, I wanted to share the One who had been with me and held me safe in His almighty hands, no matter how the tempest raged.

Just a couple of days before the event, my co-worker called to let me know I'd be speaking through a translator, another new challenge. If I was going to use any Scripture passages, I would need to turn them in ahead of time so the translator could be prepared. So the next morning I went in early to my office at Sight & Sound to allow myself some extra preparation time.

Pulling the Bible I kept there from its shelf, I leafed through it and marked down the Scripture verses I intended to include. As I turned the pages, one familiar spot to which the pages automatically fell open was the first chapter of Colossians: *"For this reason, since the day we heard about you, we have not stopped praying for you . . ."* (v. 9).

How often had I prayed that passage for each of my sons since my pastor had recommended it to me? How often had I prayed it for Charlie? I had not prayed it, I realized, since the events in the Amish schoolhouse. Slamming shut the Bible, I screamed out inwardly, *I will never pray that Scripture again!*

The strength of my own reaction shook me. I'd thought I'd found healing. I'd forgiven my son. I'd given thanks, even when I hadn't felt like it. I'd found a measure of peace and joy despite the circumstances. I was preparing to share God's love and healing with others.

But at that moment, such pain and rebellion swept over me that I could hardly breathe. I suddenly realized I was indeed still harboring unforgiveness. But not against any other human being.

God, I trusted you! I raged. *I prayed for my sons. I gave them into your hands. How could you let this happen? You could have done any one of a million things to stop Charlie that day! You broke my trust!*

How could I speak to those Japanese students, telling them God would be with them in the midst of the storms, when I was so angry at God myself? I started to slide the Bible back onto its shelf. But my hand simply would not release the book. In my heart and soul, I heard God commanding me, "Pray that Scripture right now for the three sons you still have with you."

It was like a knife piercing my heart. I cried out, "No, God, that is too hard!"

Again, I felt a gentle, loving nudge. "Pray that prayer right now."

At last, not with conviction, but out of sheer obedience, I opened the Bible again to Colossians 1:9–13 and began to pray: *"For this reason, since the day we heard about Josh, we have not stopped praying for Josh. We continually ask God to fill Josh with the knowledge of his will through all the wisdom and understanding that the Spirit gives, so that Josh may live a life worthy of the Lord and please him in every way: bearing fruit in every good work, growing in the knowledge of God, being strengthened with all power according to his glorious might so that Josh may have great endurance and patience, and giving joyful thanks to the Father, who has qualified Josh to share in the inheritance of his holy people in the kingdom of light. For he has rescued Josh from the dominion of darkness and brought Josh into the kingdom of the Son he loves."*

I prayed the prayer again, replacing the pronouns with *Zach,* then *Jon.* As I finished my third time through, I felt such a sweet peace wash over me. Bowing my head, I prayed, *Heavenly Father, I do not understand you. I do not understand your ways. I do not understand why you allowed all this to happen—even though I've seen you bring good from it. No, I do not understand. But I will choose to trust you! Even if I never understand this side of heaven your reasons, I choose to trust you!*

To this point, I'd taken comfort in the fact that I was a survivor. I'd survived disability, miscarriage, death of loved ones, cancer, and now the worst that life could throw at a mother. I'd gone on with life. I'd learned and grown and matured through adversity.

181

Yes, I was a survivor. But I learned that day that it is not enough simply to survive the storms. It is in *surrender* that true peace and healing are found. I chose that day to bow my head, intentionally and obediently surrendering my anger and confusion, my need to find answers, the arrogance of my unforgiveness against the Maker of this universe who holds all our lives in His hands—including my own, Charlie's, those Amish families'—and whose good and perfect purposes for His creation cannot be thwarted by any human action.

In all the years since that day, I've never found the answers I demanded. But in surrendering to the heavenly Father who'd been with me through every storm and who had not, after all, abandoned me in this one, I've come to know such peace. I've experienced so much joy and love. I do not need to understand. I just have to trust that God *is* love and that His love is the overarching factor that governs all events on this planet and every day of my life. Someday we *will* understand.

When I finally shared my story with those Japanese students, I found out that several had friends among the group who'd brought the crane mobile to the Amish schoolhouse a few months earlier. My presentation may not have been that of a polished platform speaker, but it was from my heart. Through the translator, Japanese students shared in turn how deeply they'd been touched by my story. That became the first of countless opportunities over the next years to share my journey through storms and adversity to joy and surrender.

19

Anniversary

Though the fig tree does not bud and there are no grapes on the vines, though the olive crop fails and the fields produce no food, though there are no sheep in the pen and no cattle in the stalls, yet I will rejoice in the LORD, I will be joyful in God my Savior.

—Habakkuk 3:17–18

Anniversary Letter From Chuck and Terri to the Amish

September 27, 2007

Dear _____,

As we are approaching the anniversary of this fateful day, there is much emotion that enters our thought processes. We still have unanswered questions. We still deal with the not knowing why this took place. I must say that

183

the name you have given it, "The Happening," has been a comfort to us. The sting of the severity of the incident has been taken away somewhat by the way all of you have responded. We know that each of you deals daily with reminders and sorrows, some of which will always be with you. The fact that we are all going on in our daily lives is a tribute to our God who gives us grace and mercy beyond human understanding.

Each of you has become a testimony to us and to the world. The forgiveness you show in no way minimizes our understanding of the heartache inside. As the year progressed and we were able to get to know each of you just a little, it has helped in our healing and we believe also in yours. Your families are dear to our hearts. We so appreciate how you have allowed us to be a part of your lives in this restorative process. Moments of sorrow are often lifted by our remembrance of each of you and the prayers of so many.

Your coming to our home this past summer was a great joy to us. That day will be forever etched in our hearts. As time goes on, we hope we will have occasion to gather again. The tea with your girls was a precious time for me, and they seemed to enjoy it very much. I look forward to it being a yearly event. Perhaps in November we could have a tea for the ladies while the children are in school. It helps so to get together and talk. Our communication isn't frequent, but it is very meaningful to us.

We will be away next week but will be keeping you lifted in prayer. Habakkuk 3:17–18: "Though the fig tree does not bud and there are no grapes on the vines, though the olive crop fails and the fields produce no food, though there are no sheep in the pen and no cattle in the stalls, *yet I will rejoice in the Lord, I will be joyful in God my Savior.*"

We thank the Lord for the gracious friendship you have offered us. Our thoughts and prayers are with you always,

Chuck and Terri Roberts

❖

When it comes to my family, I worry about problems. I mull them over. I want to fix them. Make sense of them. Which makes me, I guess—a mother! I had come to peace and surrender. I no longer doubted God's love or my heavenly Father's ability to redeem human evil to His own good purposes.

But my mind still picked at the why of what Charlie had done. It was beyond my ability to grasp how a human mind could even envision, much less carry out, such things. I would mull over memories of my son from before the tragedy and try to figure out how or at what point his mind could have started separating from a normal way of thinking to becoming so depraved.

One event that came to mind was a school shooting at Platte Canyon High School in Bailey, Colorado, just five days before my son took his life and others'. I wondered if this was where Charlie had gotten the idea. I'd read commentary that if the news didn't portray so much about an incident, perhaps there would not be so many copycats. The parent in me wanted to believe Charlie had not been carrying these thoughts long-term. But when I checked details with the state police, I discovered that my son had purchased the items used in the attack well before the Platte Canyon incident.

I found myself scrutinizing other such events. Years later, Adam Lanza, the young man who perpetrated the Sandy Hook school shootings, would be among those I analyzed. I saw certain common denominators. Like my son, many of the perpetrators had struggled with severe learning disabilities. They were introverts, quiet and withdrawn at times.

Most had come from normal, caring homes and had been normal, well-behaved, even affectionate children. How does a person turn from a happy child to a man capable of atrocity? Several such perpetrators had been diagnosed as bipolar or schizophrenic. My son had been at a typical age for such disorders to emerge. Had his quietness those last years masked darker symptoms? Do such mental debilities stem from physical pain, mental stress, emotional trauma, physical trauma—or a combination of all of these?

When I thought of physical and emotional stress, I thought back to those first months of unraveling casts from Charlie's club feet and hearing him scream. What effect could that have left on him? In more recent years, I've met and prayed with people struggling with just such dark thoughts and mental disorders. How many people out there are in such deep darkness that they simply cannot see the light? How much of such darkness is spiritual, and how much is mental and physical malady?

I have not found answers, nor am I knowledgeable enough to address such issues. But I want to understand the pain within a mentally disturbed mind and to do whatever is within my grasp to pull those drowning in darkness toward the light. At the same time, I'm not one to look back and find excuses for wrongdoing. Life can too easily become a game of blaming our decisions on outside factors. Whether driven by rage and despondency or acting intentionally, we are responsible for our actions. Whatever the darkness into which my son and others descended, I believe that for each there came a moment when they had opportunity to turn away from evil or to embrace it.

Such a moment was described by the surviving Amish girls when Charlie asked them to pray for him. My heart still breaks that he did not choose differently at that moment. My heart aches for family members currently struggling to recognize and cope with such mental and emotional sickness in a loved one. May we as a society come together to give better support to our neighbors who are dealing with such situations. If even one more Nickel Mines, Platte Canyon, or Sandy Hook tragedy can thereby be prevented, it will be worth the investment.

Though I could not keep my mind from returning to such questions, I made every effort to keep them from dominating my thoughts and my life. The bond of friendship that the Amish had extended to our family had become my greatest comfort as the months went on. I wanted to do something to show my appreciation and gratitude. Lancaster County was experiencing beautiful summer weather that July of 2007, so I thought of a picnic in our backyard. My sister, Jean, who lived adjacent to us, had a nice outdoor pool. I knew that was one amenity the Amish families did not have accessible to them.

While I was excited about my idea, I wasn't so sure the Amish families would feel the same. I asked several of them if they felt such an invitation would be appropriate. They were enthusiastic, so I sent out invitations. At Amish get-togethers, it is the custom for everyone to bring along all kinds of delicacies. But I wanted this to be our treat, so I asked them to bring only swimsuits for the children.

To my delight, every family who'd had a son or daughter in the schoolhouse agreed to come. The day of the picnic dawned warm, but perfect. What excitement I felt as a yellow school bus and three vans filled with Amish pulled into our driveway. Among the arrivals was six-year-old Rosanna in her wheelchair. Pastor Dwight and his family, our son Josh and his wife, my sister, Jean, and her husband, along with a few friends, all joined us.

We proceeded to the backyard. Following Amish tradition, the women gathered in one area of the yard, the men on the other side. The food we'd set out was ordinary picnic fare along with fresh fruits and salads. I asked if we could pray a blessing over the meal. One of the fathers immediately asked that we respect their tradition of silent prayer, so we did.

Our backyard was soon alive with chatter and laughter. The boys quickly jumped into the pool. The girls in their sky-blue, purple, and green dresses ran around playing croquet and other games. I joined the women. I still had difficulty matching all the names to faces I'd seen that first day at the Bart fire hall, but I'd come to know the mothers at least through our family visits. I remember visiting with the mother of Esther, one of the survivors. I'd discovered she was a single mother. Her husband had been killed sometime earlier in an accident. *How much can one family endure?* I grieved. But she was pleasant and smiling as she told me how Esther's injuries continued to heal.

Rosanna looked so sweet and pretty cuddled in her mother's arms. I asked Mary Liz if I could hold her. She immediately settled Rosanna on my lap. I sang to her one of the songs I sing to my grandchildren. The movement of her eyes and her smile indicated some response.

If I'd wondered whether the outing was a good idea, by day's end it was abundantly clear the entire group was enjoying the interaction as much as I was. A special blessing was to see Chuck, as well as my son Josh and his wife, Keturah, laughing and talking with our visitors. As the Amish families prepared to leave, one of the boys, Aaron Jr., who at age thirteen had been the oldest boy in the schoolhouse, came up to me.

"Mrs. Roberts, thank you for inviting me to your home," he said with a huge smile on his face. "I had so much fun."

If he only knew how much that statement meant to me that evening! To think that this young man who'd undergone such turmoil due to the actions of my son could come to the home in which Charlie had been raised and say to his mother, "I had so much fun." What a healing moment it was for me, and I hope it was for him as well. God would eventually use Aaron Jr. in a very special way in my own life as well as others'. I am so thankful to have met him personally that day.

It was well after dark before our guests piled back into the school bus and vans. We waved our good-byes, knowing this was not an ending, but the beginning of relationships that would extend well into our future.

My next interaction was actually prompted by the picnic. It hadn't occurred to me in my planning that girls do not swim with boys in the Amish culture. Watching the boys frolicking around my sister's pool, I determined the girls should not have to miss such a fun experience. My mind flashed to a formal tea a dear friend had hosted to cheer me up when I was going through cancer. What if I hosted such a tea just for the girls?

So a few weeks later, in August, I invited over all the girls from the new Amish schoolhouse—the five survivors as well as the new transferees. I borrowed an octagonal table and fancy tablecloth, which I set up in the sun-room. The table was set with antique vases filled with fresh flowers, cloth napkins and cherub napkin rings, fine china and fancy teapots. A friend of mine, Anne Petersheim, had researched each of the girls' birth dates. She purchased china cups and saucers engraved with each girl's birth month. My sister, Jean, and her daughter Serena pitched in to make goodies. Anne Petersheim and my friend Delores volunteered as clean-up crew.

Once again we enjoyed perfect weather with an ever so slight breeze and a not-too-humid, warm day. All the girls except one were able to come, along with their teacher, Emma Mae, and one of the mothers. My own mother came as well. None of the Amish girls had been to a formal tea. Their eyes grew wide as they took in the tables and fancy dishes.

I'd based my menu on an English afternoon high tea. Peach Mango and English Breakfast teas steamed in the teapots. We began with a fresh fruit cup. Next the girls had a choice of chilled cucumber or cantaloupe soup. Then came an array of tea sandwiches—tomato/cucumber, carrot/beet, mock-salmon, egg-and-olive, strawberry cream cheese, and peanut butter and jelly. Topping off the menu were mouth-watering English scones served with clotted cream, an assortment of jams, and home-made lemon curd.

The girls were a little uncertain over some of the unfamiliar fare offered, but they sampled it all graciously and devoured the more familiar peanut butter and jelly sandwiches and scones. They were excited to discover they'd be able to take their own teacup and saucer home. They were just as excited to jump into the pool. Such giggles and joyful sounds came from the bedrooms as they changed into their swimming gear. Such long, beautiful hair and so many hairpins!

Rosanna had come later than the rest after her physical therapy. I was touched by the love and concern the other girls showed Rosanna, always making sure to include her in what was going on. Though she napped through much of the tea party, she woke up enough to be a part of the swim party. Holding her in my arms so that she could dangle her feet in the water, I sang her one of the lullabies I'd sung to my own children and grandchildren. I will never forget her smile as I sang. Or hearing for the first time her soft, delighted chuckle at the antics of my sister Jean's daughter Serena, who'd joined the Amish girls in the pool. Or the singing of the other little girls as they splashed, as sweet as an angel chorus.

Oh, the joy I felt that day in seeing such normal behaviors exhibited by these precious girls who'd undergone so much trauma less than a year before. Could our heavenly Father really provide so much healing in such a short time? The evidence was before my eyes.

My heart overflowed with rejoicing and thankfulness that day. Thankfulness for the special time we had experienced. Thankfulness for parents who were willing to allow their precious daughters to come to our home. Thankfulness for how God was continuing to work in all our lives to take what should not have been and bring about something good and new.

Our girls' tea became an annual tradition for the next five years. When we finally quit, it was because the girls were growing up. One by one, they graduated from school and went on to jobs and new lives. Though I hated to see the tradition end, I recognized that season of life had ended for the girls and for me.

20

Rosanna

My grace is sufficient for you, for my power is made
perfect in weakness.

—2 Corinthians 12:9

Another tradition begun that year continues on to this day.
The first anniversary of the shooting came and went. As we'd
expected, the date brought a fresh flurry of media attention.
We received constant requests for interviews while media vans
again became a familiar sight around our property. As a family, we chose once again to leave town, this time with Marie's
new husband, Dan, and his children and mother included. As
before, it was not only a wonderful distraction for both children
and adults, but allowed us to associate positive new memories
together as a family with this difficult time of year.

Shortly after our return, I planned another tea, this time for
the mothers of the Amish schoolhouse children, not only of the

girls involved but also of the boys. Ten of the mothers attended along with my own mother, my daughter-in-law Marie, and those friends who'd helped with the girls' tea—Anne, Delores, my sister, Jean, as well as my sister-in-law, Barb. Cheri Lovre was in town, and she stopped by with Linda Shoemaker, the grief counselor who'd been so helpful to our family and was now guidance counselor to Marie and Charlie's children at their new elementary school.

As the women arrived, my usual fear of not remembering names gave me some anxiety. But they were all so gracious that my nervousness quickly ebbed. One of the women brought a beautiful bouquet; others, gifts of a book or treats to share. Rosanna's mother, Mary Liz, had brought her homegrown dried-mint meadow tea, a special treat. I in turn had chosen some favorite teas that differed from the norm—Walnut Green, Bluebells Black, Winter Punch, Mistletoe Red. Along with similar goodies as we'd prepared for the girls' tea, I brought out my crepe maker. We filled the fresh crepes with Nutella, bananas, strawberries, and blueberries.

What a delightful time we had sampling the different teas and goodies. The Amish mothers' chatter held such charm and joy that it was difficult to conceive on this bright day the tragedy that had brought us all together. And now, only one year later, here I was—who'd never before known personal relationships among the Amish—and all these mothers—who'd experienced so much loss—gathered together. We sat around a table in the beautiful sun-room Amish builders had made possible, enjoying each other's company as though we'd all been friends for many years. Truly only God's love and forgiveness could make possible such a tableau.

After our tea, we gathered in a circle. I asked each woman to share her high points and low points of the previous year.

Despite the lightheartedness of our teatime, there was no su-
garcoating how difficult the past year had been. The mothers
shared openly moments of hardship, but also of joy and healing.
Can anything be more precious than time spent with women
who've endured pain and yet hold eternal hope in their hearts?

One comment shared by Rosanna's mother, Mary Liz, particularly gripped my heart. In speaking of her low point, she
shared how different her situation was from the others'. The
other mothers who'd lost children could turn to each other
for consolation. The mothers of survivors had watched their
daughters heal. Only she was struggling with the burden of a
daughter who still lived, but was not returning to normal and
whose ongoing needs were so many and so difficult.

Ever since I'd held Rosanna in the pool, I'd ached to do
something more for this beautiful little girl and her sorrowing
family. I could only imagine what a strain her daily care was
on them. As the mothers gathered their wraps to leave, I approached Mary Liz. Would she mind if I came to spend some
time with Rosanna? Perhaps read and sing to her once a week?
I asked with diffidence, because I wasn't sure Rosanna's mother
would want the mother of her daughter's attacker in her home
on a regular basis. But Mary Liz responded with unhesitating
appreciation. We settled on my coming the following Thursday
to spend the evening with Rosanna. Eight years later, I am still
visiting at regular intervals.

A few months later, in February 2008, we scheduled one more
tea for the grandmothers who'd also been through so much loss.
We planned it at a time when Cheri Lovre could be in town.
Cheri and her colleague Linda Shoemaker had offered to prepare
a special meal from Cheri's home country, Czechoslovakia. The
main dish was dumplings with cabbage and pork chops. For
dessert, Cheri prepared *kolache*, a traditional Eastern European

holiday pastry with a poppy seed filling. Linda added a German cake with a warm lemon sauce.

This time the weather was terrible, a wintry mix of sleet and snow threatening to cancel our gathering. But these stouthearted Amish grandmothers were not daunted. As the group arrived, shaking water and ice crystals from their black wraps, my heart rejoiced that they'd been willing to weather such a storm to accept my hospitality. Their indomitable attitude was to me an embodiment of a confident spirit that chooses to move forward, refusing to be crushed by life's harsh interruptions.

The grandmothers loved Cheri's special dishes—not so dissimilar to their own German cooking—and the family history behind the meal. Again, we followed our feast with a sharing time. These older women had so much wisdom. Several mentioned the Bible passage I'd shared at the fire hall (Philippians 4:6–8) and how much its message of thanksgiving and peace in God had meant to them. Cheri asked them to sing, and they raised their voices in some of their beautiful Amish hymns. Once again tears mingled with rejoicing and fellowship. The grandmothers stayed long past the scheduled pickup time, and it was with reluctance that we finally all said our good-byes, the grandmothers pulling on their black wraps, so identical I couldn't see how they could possibly know which one was their own.

While the grandmothers' tea has not continued, the mothers' tea has become an ongoing tradition every year in October. We try out new teas, new variations of crepes, and share the highlights of our year. When transportation arrives to take my guests home, my heart is warmed by exclamations of "Oh no, it's time to leave? The driver is here already?"

But back to another ongoing tradition that has become a precious part of my weekly routine over the last years. When I arrived at the King home that initial Thursday evening, my first query was what I could do with Rosanna that would be most helpful to Mary Liz and her husband, Christ (pronounced like the first half of Christian). They were such a caring, vibrant young family with three active boys—Leroy, age nine; three-year-old Alvin; and baby Johnny—as well as their severely disabled daughter. Mary Liz had shared how difficult it had become for the rest of the family to sit down for an evening meal with Rosanna's restlessness and constant need for supervision. So I volunteered to take care of Rosanna's needs so the rest of the family could enjoy an undisturbed evening.

This proved more difficult than I'd anticipated. Rosanna's beautiful little frame was dead weight, awkward to lift and position. Her body was stiff, her head listing constantly to the far left, hands drawn in so tightly that it was impossible to pull her fingers apart. Rolled-up socks had to be placed inside her curled-up fists to keep her fingernails from cutting into her palms. Her care included diaper changes, pouring nutrients down a feeding tube, grabbing for a bucket set close by when a stomach reaction caused her to expel her food.

Even harder was witnessing her restlessness, hearing her cry out as though in anguish. Part of the evening routine involved putting her through exercises on her quadriciser, a physical therapy machine that moves all four limbs. This clearly distressed her. My heart joined her cries of anguish. The realization that her suffering had been caused by my son's actions felt more than I could bear.

Had God truly prompted me to offer this service? I feared not. I feared that I could not carry this out. That I might be doing more harm than good in coming here.

But I had committed myself. Next week would be better, I assured myself firmly. I'd taken along one of my children's favorite read-aloud stories, *Charlotte's Web*. When Rosanna's evening routine was finished, I opened its pages. As I read about a pig named Wilbur and his selfless spider friend Charlotte who lived on a farm not so dissimilar to this one, I couldn't be sure Rosanna's occasional smile meant she understood. But her brothers gathered close to listen eagerly.

I made it through the evening. But driving home from the Kings', I found myself spilling buckets of tears as I had not in weeks. *God, what do you want me to do?* I cried out. *If I am to do this—and I felt so sure that you, God, were calling me to be with this child—then I need your strength. My strength is not enough. I cannot handle this on my own!*

The next Thursday was about the same, though with fewer surprises since I now knew Rosanna's routine. Rosanna was restless with me, and I left unsure whether or not I could continue. Could I bear to come away each week with such a heavy heart? But my heart's desire was also to honor my commitment, and however difficult, I felt sure God was calling me to continue. Instead of quitting, I committed to praying unceasingly for this precious little girl. As I entered my garage that evening, I remained in the car, crying out, *I cannot do this in my own strength. If you want me to continue, it has to be your strength, God! You show strength through my weakness.*

The third week I saw those prayers answered as Rosanna and I spent a wonderful evening together. She handled the full twenty-five minutes of her quadriciser routine, her little frame far less rigid than in prior weeks. I sang and read to her. Once again, Rosanna's brothers gathered around to enjoy the adventures of Wilbur and Charlotte. I drove home that evening without shedding a tear.

Those first weeks have now turned into years. Each Thursday evening, I look forward to my time with Rosanna. I have come to love this little girl as my own granddaughter. Christ and Mary Liz, along with Rosanna's brothers (a fourth son, Benuel, has since been added to the family), have become like family. Rosanna's healing has been slow and limited. She is more relaxed, especially her hands, which no longer need rolled-up socks tucked under her fingers. She smiles and giggles and shows attentiveness when I make up silly songs for her or put dramatic expression into the stories I read. She shows recognition of the people in her life. Sometimes when she cries out, it seems she is striving to express her own thoughts and words.

But Rosanna is still unable to communicate, move around, or even eat as others do. My cry to God has been that Rosanna would be restored to a healthy childhood. But that has not been the case. Early in my time with Rosanna, I remember her mother stating bravely, "Perhaps God has allowed this for Rosanna to be a constant reminder of that day."

I for one cannot claim to understand in the smallest measure God's reasons or purpose for what has become of Rosanna's life. But what I know beyond any wavering or doubt is that God's love has never abandoned her. After we finished *Charlotte's Web*, I began reading *Anne of Green Gables*. One line in the story described Anne as having a look of silent hope. I remember looking down into Rosanna's sweet face.

"You are that little girl with the look of silent hope," I told her.

And so she is. Today, all these years later, the little girl whom doctors sent home to die is now a teenager. There is nothing easy about her life. If there has been improvement, it has too often been three steps forward and two back. Her parents continue to bear more responsibility and stress than any parent should have to bear. But Rosanna lives each day surrounded by love—not just from her own family, but the greater Amish community and others who are blessed to come and visit her. Though she cannot speak, her beautiful smile and joyful laugh radiate back the spirit of love, peace, and hope that fills her home.

My experience with Rosanna has been a most enriching portrayal of life not as it should have been but as it is. It is truly a lesson for each of us in taking what life has to offer and making the most of it. I consider myself so privileged to be part of her life. Whenever I share my story, I plead prayers for Rosanna. *Oh, Rosanna, will you ever walk again on this earth, or wait for streets of gold?*

Whatever God's ultimate plan for this precious young woman, I cling to trust that my earliest prayers after "The Happening" will be answered, that our Amish friend's statement concerning the events of October 2, 2006, will be true in Rosanna's life individually. However tragic and unfair Rosanna's current situation, our heavenly Father *will* bring about good from evil. Rosanna's life *will* be a beacon of light in a dark world. If Rosanna is truly to be a living reminder of that day, let it not be a reminder of tragedy and evil's triumph. Let it be instead of divine love, forgiveness, compassion, redemption, the beauty God can create from the dingiest and darkest ashes.

I pray the same for her schoolmates. Despite their sweet smiles and laughter when I see them, returning to a new normal has not always been a smooth road for the other survivors either. Each of the girls has had hardships and sorrows to bear. There have been continuing surgeries to deal with the aftereffects of the wounds they received. Care continues to be provided by funds contributed by so many compassionate people around the world. But there remain ongoing needs. There is more information at the end of the book for those interested in making a donation. May God's love, comfort, and healing continue to touch each of these precious lives as they move forward into young adulthood.

21

A Spacious Place

He brought me out into a spacious place; he rescued me
because he delighted in me.

—Psalm 18:19

And so one year passed. Then another. The new normal began
to seem—well, normal! For the most part, our small corner
of Lancaster County, Pennsylvania, had disappeared from the
world stage. Each anniversary of the event brought a dimin-
ishing flurry of media attention. Still, with each fall, a tension
would build up inside me. Not even a conscious tension. But
once the anniversary passed, I'd realize I'd been holding my
breath for days. The sweet release of that tension would remind
me I'd survived another year.

No, I'd surrendered another year. However devastating this
life tsunami had once appeared, it seemed at last to have ebbed

out to sea. My new normal of work, family, visiting Rosanna and others of the Amish community was now familiar and comfortable.

Within our family, life went on as well. Zach brought us a beautiful new Swedish daughter-in-law, Karin. He and Josh and Jon each blessed us with more grandchildren. Marie and Dan kept us always involved in the activities of their blended family. With each passing year, my heart rejoiced more that I had not, after all, lost a beloved daughter-in-law and grandchildren, but truly gained a new son.

More children were born as well to the Amish schoolhouse families. Chuck and I remained in contact, celebrating each new birth. Nickel Mines scholars have now graduated and gone on to apprenticeships, jobs, even become teachers. Some have married.

I could not pinpoint the moment I realized that every thought of my waking day and sleeping dreams no longer centered on the events of October 2, 2006. Perhaps it was a drive through the woods more than two years later. From the earliest days after Charlie's death, I hadn't been able to drive through a wooded mountainous area without a feeling of foreboding and melancholy. I would take a nature walk along a stream, planning to spend time praising my heavenly Father for the beauty of His creation. Instead my thoughts would go to my firstborn, who had so loved the outdoors. Once again I'd catch myself mulling over unanswered questions. *Oh, Charlie, you loved all this so! How could you possibly leave it and all the precious memories you could have shared with your children?*

Praying did not banish my feelings. Instead I chose to avoid situations and settings that could evoke such thoughts. Then one day it happened. I was on a business trip to Branson, Missouri, where Sight & Sound Theatres maintains a second production complex. My drive from the airport involved more than two hours on back roads through mountainous areas by myself in a rental car. The day was bright and clear, the forest-cloaked hillsides a splendid demonstration of divine artistry. I was approaching Branson when I suddenly realized I'd truly enjoyed the drive. Charlie had not entered my mind, only the beauty of God's creation.

The sticky warmth of a grandchild's hug. Laughter at a good friend's joke. A beach stroll with sea salt in my nostrils and wind in my hair. The red-and-gold flicker of flames dancing in my sun-room's fireplace with snow falling softly outside the glass. The murmur of family members opening Christmas gifts. When did such moments as these begin to overshadow pain and grief? Cheri Lovre was right. My tear bucket would never be empty. But life's special moments, the happiness of ordinary days, the peaceful tenor of passing weeks, months, and years increasingly outweighed those flashes of remembered sorrow.

One aspect of my new normal continued to astonish me. Increasingly, I was being asked to share my story, often in churches, as well as with senior citizen groups, students, and other civic organizations. That my experience of redemptive love and forgiveness could bring healing and forgiveness to others was not something I'd foreseen. But so it proved. Even more astonishing was to find myself sharing that message side by side and hand in hand with the very Amish families my son had harmed.

My first such event was at a small Lancaster area church. Enough chairs had been set up for an anticipated attendance of perhaps twenty to twenty-five women. I could not help wondering if anyone would show up for such a distressing subject. To my surprise, the chairs quickly filled up. More were brought in until at least seventy to eighty were seated. I was still not a polished speaker. But I spoke from my heart of my own journey in finding joy through adversity. Of my greatest life storms:

cancer and Charlie. Of the urgency of surrendering bitterness and not stuffing it inside to eat away at heart and soul and mind as my son had done. Of the healing that came through choosing forgiveness above vengeance, love instead of hate.

More invitations poured in, not only locally, but for out-of-state conferences and retreats. Each retelling of my story was a painful dredging up of memories. But if that retelling could positively touch even one life, I could not allow my own discomfort to interfere. Still, I never anticipated the level of response I encountered. One teenage girl approached me to share how angry she'd been with God for letting her father die of cancer when she was twelve years old. But she was choosing to forgive God. In another church, a woman came who'd been hostile to hearing my story. A friend had encouraged her to come. She came up afterward to offer a heartfelt thank-you for the healing my message had brought to her spirit. After a breakfast event for several hundred women, a young mother in her thirties shared with me of her husband's brain cancer.

"Your message of forgiveness has helped me let go of my anger with God over my husband's pain," she told me. "Like you, I don't understand God's reasons. But I will choose to trust and have faith."

Another mother approached me with her son, who'd endured the unspeakable horror of having to witness his mother being raped. She'd found forgiveness, but he had not, and she was so grateful that her son had been able to hear my story. I pray that young man has at last released that hurt.

Above all, it became increasingly clear to me how great a need there is in this world for such a message of forgiveness. So many I met were hurting so deeply. I found myself returning again and again to another familiar passage, 2 Corinthians 1:3–4:

Praise be to the God and Father of our Lord Jesus Christ, the Father of compassion and the God of all comfort, who comforts us in all our troubles, so that we can comfort those in any trouble with the comfort we ourselves receive from God.

My compassionate heavenly Father has poured His comfort into my life. And though sharing my story has never become easy, I count myself privileged to share with others who are facing trouble the comfort I myself have so abundantly received.

Early on, only rarely did any of the Amish parents accompany me as I spoke. But on one of those first speaking engagements, one of the Amish mothers, Anna Mary, volunteered to come with me. While her culture didn't permit her to participate on the platform, her presence offered strength and support.

Then in May 2009, I received a call from two of the Amish fathers, Amos and John. A Canadian film crew wanted to do a piece on forgiveness relating to an incident in their own country that would have its twentieth anniversary that year. The Amish culture, with its strong emphasis on never glorifying self but only God, strongly discouraged anything that would draw personal attention, whether on camera or a platform.

"Since we will not participate in this," Amos and John told me, "we'd like you to tell your story."

Wow! I wasn't so sure either about finding myself on the opposite end of a film camera. But I agreed to the interview, and when the documentary came out, I was happy to see the emphasis on these Amish families' display of forgiveness. Several books and movies concerning the Nickel Mines shooting would be released, among them Don Kraybill's *Amish Grace*, which included a print interview of me, and a follow-up movie by the same name. I rejoiced to see the theme of forgiveness made central in each retelling, although it took time to be accepting of some of these public portrayals.

/ In March 2010, I received another call from one of the Amish parents. A few months earlier in Mont Vernon, New Hampshire, four young men ages seventeen to twenty had broken into a randomly chosen home, where in a thrill killing they'd brutally murdered a mother, leaving her eleven-year-old daughter for dead, while the father was out of town. The killers all came from prosperous, upstanding families, one of them a homeschooler. The machete and knife injuries inflicted on mother and daughter had been so gruesome, the young killers showing no remorse for their deeds, that this small New Hampshire town of only two thousand residents had been left stunned. Community tensions were running high with a lot of anger, grief, and calls for vengeance. A local pastor had contacted the Nickel Mines Amish, asking if they'd be willing to share their experience of loss and forgiveness with the Mont Vernon community. Would I be willing to accompany them and share my story?

In the end, both Chuck and I participated in the trip. Twelve of us filled up a large van: eight Amish schoolhouse parents, the area Amish bishop and his wife, me, and Chuck as the van driver. It proved a difficult, but eminently worthwhile experience. We met with the parents of the perpetrators, as well as with community leaders who were struggling to deal with the ongoing fear and trauma this horrific event had precipitated in a setting where residents had not even felt a need to lock their doors.

Everywhere we met with incredulity that these Amish victims could so willingly travel and share with the parents of their own perpetrator. How much impact our example and words might have had, we will never know. But we saw clearly a melding of hearts among community leaders as they listened to the Amish and me share in turn. As to the twelve of us who'd traveled together, those three days in the van were a bonding experience I will treasure forever.

By now I'd been privileged to share my message and journey of forgiveness with audiences across several states and Canada. I never expected to have such an opportunity among the Amish. But in the summer of 2011, I received a call from one of the schoolhouse parents. Extended family members from an Amish community in Ohio were visiting Lancaster County and would be attending a Sight & Sound show. They'd recently gone through a terrible ordeal when the patriarch of the family had murdered his wife and son and then taken his own life. Despite the teachings of their Amish heritage, the surviving family members were struggling with forgiveness and other ongoing emotional issues. Would I be willing to meet with them and share how God had wrought forgiveness in my own life?

I was given their family name and the time of the show they were attending. Entering into the Sight & Sound auditorium before the curtain rose, I quickly spotted two rows of gray—the traditional dress of this Ohio Amish community. I introduced myself and mentioned the mutual Amish friend who'd given me their name. It was clear they knew the significance of my name.

"Welcome to Lancaster," I told them simply, leaving them to enjoy the show. But during the intermission, they sought me out and began to pour out their story.

"How do we move forward?" they asked me. "How did you move forward?"

Again, I could only share the comfort God had given me. Our discussion was deep, but brief. The family returned to Ohio, but about a month later I received a call from John Fisher, father of little Barbie, Emma, and their older sister, Marian, who'd died in the schoolhouse. Without preamble, he asked, "Terri, what are you doing today?"

"Well, I was just heading to work," I answered. "But if you need me, I can make myself available."

John explained that more of the Ohio family had come to town, four siblings and their spouses. "They want to get together with you. May I bring them over?"

We made arrangements to meet at my home at 2 p.m. I returned home that afternoon. By the time I'd straightened up my sun-room and prepared some platters of fresh fruit, the group had arrived. There were fourteen in all, more than I'd set out chairs for, but my Amish acquaintances in the group made themselves at home, collecting chairs from other areas of the house to form a large circle. Sitting there in that peaceful room with sunbeams slanting through the windows and the beautiful panorama of the Lancaster County countryside, we talked and shared stories, not only of pain and confusion and grief, but also of forgiveness.

It was such a blessed time of fellowship, and it struck me as we all said our good-byes how improbable the outside world would find the day's events: the Amish calling the mother of the Nickel Mines schoolhouse gunman to bring healing to other Amish in pain. This could only be described as a miracle of divine grace, love, and forgiveness.

One family member had not come with the others, a married daughter who was struggling greatly with her father's actions. She'd moved from her Ohio neighborhood and had little contact with the others. I was asked if I'd speak to her on the phone. I did so and encouraged her not to shut herself off from family and friends who were reaching out to her. So much of my own healing had come through refusing to shut myself off out of shame for what Charlie had done, but allowing others who'd poured out compassion and help to be part of my life.

Later on I was invited to Ohio to speak at a business event and visit the family personally. Chuck took time out from his busy schedule to drive me. While Chuck has not actively involved himself in public speaking with me or the Amish, he is my backbone, my sounding board, the one who keeps me grounded and gives wise counsel on moving forward into new ventures. I am so thankful for his strong support of my growing speaking ministry. Chuck and I met with the family of the daughter with whom I'd spoken on the phone, and I spoke as well to two different groups.

From these contacts, an ongoing relationship with the Ohio Amish community has developed. I've been back several times since to speak at various events in the area. How wonderful to see this hurting daughter again not so long ago, now moved back into the neighborhood with her family and friends, expecting a child, and radiating peace in her heart and life.

May I encourage you, dear reader: If you are going through a tragedy, don't shut yourself off from others. It is our instinct in such situations to curl up and hide from staring eyes and accusing words. And there may be those we encounter who convey just such a negative response. But believe me, there are far more—family, friends, a local church body—eager to offer comfort and help. Oh, how I can give testimony to that! Let them in.

22

The Fifth Anniversary

Carry each other's burdens, and in this way you will fulfill
the law of Christ.

—Galatians 6:2

By fall 2011, it was hard to believe five years had already gone
by since "The Happening." It seemed that only yesterday a tsunami had uprooted my life, while at the same time that former
life seemed so distant as to belong to another woman. That the
five-year anniversary would engender a fresh flurry of media
attention and commemorative activities was to be expected,
and so it turned out.

The most significant was a symposium on forgiveness being
hosted at the Elizabethtown College campus about a half-hour
drive from the city of Lancaster. One of the event organizers,
sociologist Don Kraybill, the author of *Amish Grace*, asked me
to speak at the event. I shared the invitation with my Amish

friends. How deeply moved I was to see every one of the Nickel Mines schoolhouse families in the audience to give me support as I spoke. Amish from Ohio and Indiana were in attendance as well.

That event brought my first interaction with reporters. I'd refused so many requests for interviews over the years. But I'd seen the healing my own story of forgiveness had brought as I spoke, and I knew the time had come to share that message with a listening world. I was astonished at how many news outlets printed excerpts from those interviews, including *The Philadelphia Inquirer* and AP News Service.

At the symposium, I was approached as well by a man who ran a hotline for Old Order Mennonites. Would I be willing to do an online event for the hotline? The event was set up from my sun-room. After sharing my story, I took questions that came in from across the United States and Canada.

I also met the chaplain of the Cancer Treatment Centers of America at the symposium. "You are a poster child for the message we want to give of healing," he told me. "We've found that harboring unforgiveness makes it harder for cancer patients to heal. Letting go of bitterness and anger and learning to forgive improve physical healing as well as mental healing."

He'd written an entire book himself on the benefits of forgiveness.[1] I accepted his invitation to speak at a CTCA leadership event in Philadelphia, sharing my experiences with the living foods treatment for my cancer, as well as my usual message on forgiveness and joy through adversity.

While the Amish steadfastly refused media interviews or platform speaking, they continued to participate in a number of events that allowed them to share personally. Among these

1. Michael S. Barry, *The Forgiveness Project* (Grand Rapids, MI: Kregel, 2011).

was a meeting set up by our friend Ruth Powers with Japanese visitors who had just survived their own very tangible tsunami earlier that spring. The March 2011 9.0 Richter scale earthquake and ten-meter-high tsunami wave had also caused a meltdown of Japanese nuclear reactors, leaving the planet's worst ongoing nuclear disaster since Chernobyl.

I'd made arrangements for the group of Japanese survivors to see a live production of the story of Joseph, then playing at Sight & Sound Theatre. Ruth asked if I'd be willing to bring some of the Amish families with me to share at an informal picnic with the survivors. The interest grew so quickly that the event was moved to a large Lancaster-area church.

The Amish who'd accompanied me had been seated up front in a row of chairs facing the audience. A Japanese pastor provided translation for the Japanese contingent. I was no expert at speaking through a translator. As I spoke of my own tsunami, I was not paying attention to the occasional concerned look on the translator's face as he scrambled to keep up. I can remember vividly the Amish mother seated closest to me, now a dear friend, tugging on my skirt and whispering that I needed to slow down so the translator could catch up.

After I finished, one of the Amish fathers gave a personal testimony of forgiveness through Jesus Christ. Then the Japanese visitors were allowed to ask questions. Over and over, they expressed amazement to see the Amish parents sitting side by side with me and how deeply they were touched by the Amish community's act of forgiveness. One of the Japanese students shared how he'd first heard our story of forgiveness in his own country and shared it with others. Another Japanese woman expressed how in her culture my family would never have been able to show our faces socially again. We would have been ostracized due to the crime of our son.

Among the Amish parents who'd attended were Rosanna's dad, Christ King; Aaron and Anna Mary Esh, parents of Aaron Jr., who'd been the oldest boy in the schoolhouse; and Amos and Kate Ebersol, parents of Naomi Rose. How wonderful it was to watch them intermingling and sharing personally with the visitors. For these Amish families from such a quiet, unassuming culture that mixed so rarely with outsiders, the day's events and all the others we'd shared together were as far from the old normal as they were for me.

Around this same time, the Mennonite Central Committee (MCC) was hosting an event for international representatives, many from such war zones as Rwanda and the Congo. I'd also made arrangements for this group to get Sight & Sound tickets. The delegates wanted to meet me and the Nickel Mines Amish. This time most of the schoolhouse families were represented as we gathered at a small church near the Bart firehouse. The delegates shared their own stories of loss and tragedy from their nations' war zones. The urgency and impact of forgiveness bringing about true reconciliation and ongoing change in society became the focus of our discussion.

If to this point I'd been astounded that people wanted to hear my story, the five-year anniversary opened the doors even wider to speaking on an increasingly far-reaching scale. To date I'd shared my story at more than one hundred speaking events. In early 2012, I was invited again to Ohio, where around eight hundred Amish and "English" packed out a high school auditorium. After I spoke, the receiving line was a long one. I saw pain in so many eyes as one after another told me, "I never thought I'd be able to share this with anyone who truly understood the depth of the pain I feel."

I talked privately with an Amish family whose son had contracted his wife's murder, and then on a later trip I visited their home. The entire family gathered around the living room in a circle, perhaps thirty in all. My heart hurt at their very evident pain as we spoke.

"What can I give you for coming?" the family spokesman asked me afterward.

"I just want to be here for your family," I told him. In that moment it was as though my life story had come full circle, as much a miracle as a privilege that I could simply be there for this Amish family in need of comfort as the Amish community had been there for me and my own family not so long before.

A year or so later, I was invited to take my story internationally. My first invitation was to travel to Japan with Ruth Powers, where I spoke in four churches and two schools over a two-week period. By now I was becoming more comfortable using a translator. A highlight of that trip was to visit the Peace Child memorial, the inspiration for the thousand-cranes mobile Japanese students had brought to the makeshift Amish schoolhouse that first spring. As I stood there amidst the colorful garlands representing so many wishes, my own heart cried out that God's peace that transcends all understanding would one day spread across this planet from pole to pole.

Not long after that trip, I traveled to Peru, again speaking in churches and at women's events. At one church in the capital city of Lima, 240 women had signed up. To my surprise, more than 750 showed up. The outpouring of response I encountered in both countries was a reminder again of how universal is the need to forgive and to be forgiven.

A fresh reminder came upon my return to the United States in early 2014. By now the soft Low German accent on the phone was a familiar one. The Amish elder who'd called had a new invitation to share. It had been more than a year since the Sandy Hook Elementary School shooting, which occurred on December 14, 2012, in Newtown, Connecticut, resulting in the deaths of twenty children and six adults, as well as the gunman. But the families of the children, as well as the community, were still struggling with grief and rage. A community event addressing issues of grief counseling, healing, and forgiveness had been organized. Among a number of speakers, the Nickel Mines Amish community and I had been invited.

This time I joined thirty Amish, including four of the original Nickel Mines scholars, two boys and two girls, now young adults, to travel by bus to Newtown. One of the first responders to the schoolhouse shooting joined us. Earlier, some of this same group of Amish had visited Virginia Tech (VT) following the school shooting there, and a father of one of the VT victims also joined us. The event turnout was sizeable. I spoke twice at different times, and the Amish families shared in Q&A sessions that followed. As in Mont Vernon, we encountered incredulity at the idea—or even rightness—of forgiving a perpetrator of such evil.

What impact did we make? I truly don't know. I pray some pain was eased that day. But I remember well a conversation on the way home. By now many of my companions on the bus had heard me speak multiple times. One of them, a bishop of his Amish congregation and a man whose wisdom I'd come to respect deeply, said to me, "Terri, you left something out today in your 'joy through adversity' speech."

"What did I leave out?" I queried. It seemed he knew my message better than I did by now!

"You forgot to include what you always say about forgiveness: 'When you forgive, you don't get bitter. My son allowed bitterness to enter his heart. Don't let bitterness enter your heart. Choose to forgive.'"

I hadn't noticed I'd left it out. But I'll say it again here—and as many times as I'm given opportunity to share this urgent truth: When you forgive, there is no room in your heart for bitterness. Oh, if my son Charlie had only understood that! Don't make his mistake. Choose to forgive! Choose to think on the good things: "Whatever is true, whatever is noble, whatever is right, whatever is pure, whatever is lovely, whatever is admirable—if anything is excellent or praiseworthy—think about such things" (Philippians 4:8).

On this trip to Connecticut, I was reminded again of the incredible power of forgiveness by Kate—whose only daughter, Naomi Rose, died in the Nickel Mines schoolhouse. She told me that she prayed for me and my son on that tragic day before she even knew the condition of her daughter. That is a surrendered heart choice.

By this time another change had come into my life. As invitations to speak and travel continued to pour in, I recognized I could not at the same time effectively carry out my responsibilities at Sight & Sound Theatre. With great reluctance, in May 2013 I resigned my job. The farewell party was both fun-filled and heartrending. For twenty years, the Sight & Sound Theatre staff had been a second family. Their love and support through the tragedies of cancer and Charlie's actions had been a huge part of my physical and emotional healing. Thank you for being there for me, my wonderful Sight & Sound family!

So now I find myself rounding a new bend in my life's journey. What is around that bend? I do not know. But that I find myself looking forward to all the twists and turns the road ahead may have to offer is evidence of the healing God has wrought in my heart and soul and mind over these last years. Among the exciting new challenges have been frequent requests from those who attended my speaking events for me to pu story in written form.

Responding to that request through the pages you are now reading has necessitated reliving the events of October 2, 2006. I am confronted once more with the question my anguished heart once cried out: Can good come from evil? Has good come from evil? Has my heavenly Father, the loving Creator of heaven and earth, redeemed the wrongness of my son's choices and actions that day to bring about something beautiful from the ashes of tragedy and loss?

In answer, I find my mind going to another speaking engagement not so long ago. I'd been invited to return once again to Ohio, this time to speak at a large church. Some of its leaders had been in that school auditorium where I'd spoken to Amish and English alike in 2012, and they wanted me to share my story with their congregation. Since my husband could not go this time, a dear friend was scheduled to go with me. But at the last moment, she was not able to go.

I mentioned my disappointment and need of a traveling companion to one of the Amish mothers, Anna Mary, who had traveled with me several times to speaking events. Anna Mary and her husband, Aaron, were parents of the oldest boy who'd been in the schoolhouse that day—Aaron Jr. Thirteen years old at that time, he was now a fine young man of twenty-one. But the last years had not been easy for him. Aaron had faced his own difficult battles of grief and healing. I'd come to know Aaron well over the years. When I arrived to visit his parents that afternoon, he was standing outside.

"How are you doing?" I asked him. As we chatted about various speaking events in which his parents had participated, I added with a smile, "Hey, if you'd like to hear me speak sometime, I'd love to have you come."

I hadn't even thought of my current dilemma. But when Anna Mary regretfully explained she couldn't volunteer her own company because of a family engagement, her husband suggested, "Why don't you see if Aaron Jr. would like to go?"

By then young Aaron had left the house. But later that evening I received a call from the family saying that Aaron Jr. would be happy to accompany me to Ohio. My brother, Joe, had already volunteered to chauffeur me. So off we went.

As we traveled, I asked Aaron if he'd be willing to share briefly of his own journey of fear, faith, and forgiveness since that day in the schoolhouse. Somewhat hesitantly, he pondered the thought. But as we were driving to the church the Friday evening I was scheduled to speak, Aaron suddenly spoke up from the backseat. "Terri, I really hate that I'm going to disappoint you. But I just can't share tonight."

Turning around in the front passenger seat to look at him, I answered firmly: "First of all, there is nothing you could do to disappoint me. Just your coming along on this trip has blessed my socks off. I am honored you came. But besides, this isn't about Aaron or Terri. It's about the Holy Spirit speaking through the message. If you are meant to share, nothing will keep you in your seat. If you feel you can't share, don't feel guilty. It may not be your time yet."

I devised a simple plan. "When I get to a certain point in my talk, I'll look directly at you. If you nod 'yes,' I'll invite you up on stage. If you shake your head 'no,' I'll know it isn't your time to share."

The evening turned out to be a blustery, rainy night. Even so, several hundred braved the weather to come out. The sheer size of the crowd was enough to make anyone nervous, so it was with little expectation that I stopped partway through my message to look down at Aaron. But to my delight, he met my gaze and nodded "yes."

Excitedly, I stepped away to allow him to take my place at the microphone. At first I stood to one side, ready to step back if he had only a few comments to share. But when he began speaking of his experience and his own difficult journey to dependence on God as his heavenly Father, it was with the fervor and eloquence of a polished preacher. At last I sat down. You could have heard a pin drop in that large church sanctuary as Aaron spoke fluidly, movingly for a full twenty minutes.

As I watched the tall, blond Amish young man sharing so earnestly from his heart, it was not a victim or even a survivor I saw standing there on that platform. It was a magnificent image of God's redemptive grace, of the beauty our heavenly Father alone can bring from the ugliness of human sin and tragedy.

23

What Now?

One thing I do: Forgetting what is behind and strain-
ing toward what is ahead, I press on toward the goal to
win the prize for which God has called me heavenward
in Christ Jesus.

—Philippians 3:13–14

So I come to the end of this story, if not my life journey. As I
look back over these pages to the sun-kissed, tranquil valley
that was once my life and the tsunami that swept through it
with such brutal fury, I am left with no easy answers.

Why did my beloved firstborn son choose to do what he did
that day? I will never know this side of eternity.

Why did a loving God not reach down to prevent it? I will
not understand until one day I am blessed to glimpse the final
woven tapestry of God's purpose and plan for the human race
He created.

But here is what I do know, what I have come to understand. In my darkest night, I found the light of God's presence still with me. When a tsunami wave swept my life from its foundation, I discovered under my feet the solid rock of a faithful heavenly Father from whose loving hands no storm winds can tear me. When I made the choice to surrender pain, bitterness, anger, and unforgiveness, I gained in their place a joy and love and peace beyond all human understanding.

My dear reader, maybe you are dealing with a tragedy in your own life. Maybe you are still grappling with pain, anger, and bitterness. I cannot claim to have all the answers for you. But perhaps you will let me share just a few life lessons that have contributed greatly to my own healing.

One: Move Forward

"Moving forward" versus "moving on" has become a leitmotif of mine. Perhaps to some the two phrases may seem to hold the same meaning. But for me, moving on feels like turning my back and walking away, as in "Ya gotta let go and move on!" To move forward conveys the sense of deliberately taking one step after another while maintaining an honest perspective on lingering pain and grief.

How do you move forward when trials come, depression raises its ugly head, and you can't seem to focus? Just *take the next step*. Do the next thing that needs to be done, whether that is getting out of bed in the morning, choosing what to eat for breakfast, deciding what to wear that day. Don't worry about tomorrow or whatever else may lie ahead. Just focus on the next step. As Jesus told His disciples in Matthew 6:34: "Tomorrow will worry about itself. Each day has enough trouble of its own."

Two: Think on These Things

Part of moving forward is refusing to linger on the "if onlys."
God provides new things in our lives to bring new focus and
joy. Remaining focused on the past or what cannot be serves
no purpose in moving us forward. Introspection for the purpose of change and healing may be helpful. Introspection
that allows us to wallow in the pain and hurt is not a healthy
place to go.

As I've shared before, when those memories of what could
have been do intrude, stop and find a wonderful memory of the
person, place, or event involved. Reaffirm your thankfulness for
the good times. Then allow your mind to move forward into new
plans and new tomorrows. This includes making a conscious
effort to follow the mandate of Philippians 4:8: "Whatever is
true, whatever is noble, whatever is right, whatever is pure,
whatever is lovely, whatever is admirable—if anything is excellent or praiseworthy—think about such things."

I firmly believe that if my son had kept this verse on his lips
and in his heart every morning instead of bitterness, it would
have kept his mind from going where it did. We all have in our
lives things that are good, true, noble, and lovely, but we allow
those things to get crowded out by stresses, problems, and un-
necessary self-obsession. And when tragedy strikes, our human
instinct is to wallow in our sorrow and turn our focus inward.
Just getting our minds off ourselves and thinking of others is
a good start.

One suggestion that has greatly helped me to refocus my
thoughts in hard moments is to write out favorite Scripture
passages on index cards. When my thoughts wander to dark
places, I pull a card from my car visor while at a red light or
reread one taped to the wall in my kitchen or on my desk next

to my computer. Writing out motivational sayings or poetry selections might help as well.

Allow me to add here that I do not intend to minimize the depth of trauma the human soul can or should endure. When sorrow overwhelms you in ways that begin to gnaw at your spirit, it may be necessary and advantageous to have professional counsel intervene. I don't know how I would have coped without the wise and kind support of trauma and grief counselors Cheri Lovre and Linda Shoemaker.

Three: Practice Forgiveness

Forgiveness is the greatest healer. *It does not stop the pain.* It does not allow us to move forward effortlessly. But choosing to forgive instead of harboring bitterness is extremely freeing. My son harbored bitterness that ate away at his soul like a cancer that grows undetected. Bitterness is worse than any cancer.

Forgiveness also brings an awareness of how in our own human frailty we are capable of hurting others. It may be without intention, but even with the best intentions we can cause others pain. None of us is so perfect that we qualify to cast the first stone. When through forgiveness we take ourselves off the "victim pedestal," we release the pain that the desire for retribution causes, recognizing that as flawed human beings we are all capable of wronging another.

This does not negate punishment for wrongdoing. Had our son not taken his life, he would have been incarcerated for life, and rightly so. But how we move forward when we are wronged makes a huge difference in our ability to cope with present and future challenges.

Four: Make Right Choices

How do we respond to adversity? It's a choice we all have. We make choices every day. And our choices have consequences. Not until the events of that day was I ever so aware of how many choices we face daily in our lives and the repercussions of those choices. The choices we make in small situations will have an effect on the choices we make in bigger situations. If we choose to be fretful because a summer drizzle spoils our picnic, where will we be when a tsunami comes?

Consistently making right choices in the midst of hard times and trials builds character and gives us courage to move forward. My son made the wrong choice. The Amish families of the Nickel Mines schoolhouse made the right choice. I've been witness to the consequences of choosing unforgiveness. And I've been witness to the redemption and healing that choosing forgiveness has wrought. How different our world would be if that choice were made on a daily basis.

For myself, I choose today to surrender my emotions of fear, anger, and anxiety. I choose today to trust my heavenly Father to work out His ultimate purpose through the details of my life. I choose today forgiveness over bitterness, to return love for hate and anger.

Five: Share Your Story With Others

No one would ever invite tragedy into their life or those things that cause pain. But I've learned that the deeper the pain, the deeper the relationships we will build—with God and with other people—when we open our hearts to the healing God has for us.

Every one of us has a story to tell. Perhaps you do not relate to the particular tragedy and pain described in these pages. But you know your own personal pain. You know what wounds and scars you bear that may still be festering inside. Exposing those wounds to the light is not an easy experience, but it is a necessary step in lancing the infection and bringing about healing. And not just in your own life. As I've told my story, it has helped in my healing. But I am constantly amazed to hear how it has also helped to heal others going through trials of their own.

So tell your story. First take it to God and seek His answers and His Word in the midst of your trial. There is no one who listens better or cares more about our pain than our heavenly Father. Other human beings have so often let me down, just as I have let others down. But my heavenly Father has never forsaken me. If you personally have never experienced the love of God in your life, I encourage you to cry out to Him and ask Him to reveal His loving presence to you. I pray that everyone reading these pages may find the peace that transcends all understanding that I have found through faith in my loving God and heavenly Father.

Seek out as well at least one close confidant or mentor who can prayerfully guide you through this time. And finally, as you begin to heal, and even in the midst of your healing, share your story with others whom God brings into your life, including the comfort and healing with which you have been blessed. Perhaps someone is waiting for your story to begin their healing.

Six: Communicate, Communicate, Communicate!

Communication, though painful at times, is worth the effort. Even when our communication is not verbal, it offers common ground to comfort one another. I think back to those early days when words sometimes felt too hard. Just being with a family member or friend was comforting in so many ways.

In communicating, be willing to take the initiative. Go ahead and ask your adult child or other family member how they are doing or how you might pray for them. There was a time I worried that I might be seen as interfering. But this isn't meddling. It's letting others know you care.

Depression or mental unbalance such as my son suffered can be hidden. I remember when termites invaded our home, doing years of damage without showing themselves. There were subtle signs, ignored. I battled odd, flying ants but didn't question their source. By the time the damage was apparent to the naked eye, a large area of our house had been infested. Likewise cancer can grow unnoticed for years. My signs were less energy, small lumps, even an unexplainable toothache. By the time a doctor brought the cancer to my attention, much damage had been done to my body. With my son, I saw sadness, but I did not question it. He was an adult. I didn't want to be pushy or interfere. How I wish now that I had.

Should this make us paranoid about ourselves or those around us? No. Nor should we seek to place blame on ourselves or others for not spotting the signs or intervening in time. We can never force anyone to open up about heart matters. In my son's case, I do not know if more communication might have made a difference. But a simple searching question may be an opening into the spirit of someone battling feelings of inadequacy, despair, or darkness. I'm still not an expert at this, but I am more aware of the importance of communication. Making a deliberate effort has provided some great insights and conversation among my own family members.

Seven: Pray With Thanksgiving

Like forgiveness, a thankful heart is in itself a healing balm to the soul. On any given day we will experience good things and bad things, just as in our lives we experience good seasons and bad. If we choose to be thankful for the good things, it will raise our awareness of things for which to be thankful. If we focus instead on the negative, we will be pulled down into bitterness and darkness.

I have learned that choosing to give thanks is not the natural thing to do, but it is the necessary thing, and it releases some of the pain inside us. When life feels too hard, finding something for which to be thankful has lifted my heavy heart and given me strength to move forward. My goal each day is to find at least one specific thing for which to give thanks. Today I awoke and saw sunshine. On a cold winter night, I enjoyed a warm bed. My hopes for Charlie's future have been dashed, but I can offer thanks that my hopes for his family are being fulfilled. Seeing my grandchildren thriving, with two wonderful parents guiding them, gives me so much cause for thanksgiving. Seeing the Amish schoolhouse families move forward and thrive in their lives is a sincere desire fulfilled, and I thank God for them.

As I give thanks, I discover that my reasons for thankfulness far outnumber my reasons for sadness. And that too is a reason for thankfulness.

Eight: Focus on Eternity

My dad recently went to heaven. We ended his service with a song titled "Big House." His grandchildren played the instruments and vocalized the song that talks of a grand celebration in a mansion with lots of rooms, food, and fun.

When I shared during the service, I asked that all would realize that the final song is an invitation that requires a response. None of us are forced to accept the call to eternity that God speaks of in John 3:16: "For God so loved the world that he gave his one and only Son, that whoever believes in him shall not perish but have eternal life."

Dad is enjoying eternal life without the pain and sorrow of this world. You are invited to join him. I encourage you to make that choice now to surrender your sin for God's joy. I made that choice as a young mother raising four sons, looking for a firm foundation. I got on my knees, admitted my sin, and gave my life totally to the Lord.

Knowing we will experience eternity with God doesn't take away all the sorrow of this earth, but it does bring a peace that "transcends all understanding" (Philippians 4:7). And we know that God will never leave us or forsake us, even in a tsunami. In the midst of your storm, I encourage you to surrender your life to the Lord, knowing that no matter what this life holds, your eternal future is secure with Him.

Epilogue

A Rainbow Covenant

Whenever the rainbow appears in the clouds, I [God] will
see it and remember the everlasting covenant between
God and all living creatures of every kind on the earth.
—Genesis 9:16

Not long ago, I took a stroll through the fields behind my home
with my granddaughter Dagmar. Almost three years old, Dagmar is the daughter of Zach and Karin, who were in town for
a visit. As we meandered along, I noticed black clouds and the
smell of dampness in the air.

"Honey, we have to go inside," I told Dagmar. "A storm
is coming."

She was disappointed and reluctant to leave her exploration. I
coaxed her inside with a promise. "Look, if we go inside before

the rain comes, then when it's over, we'll come back outside and look for a rainbow."

That was all it took. She skipped and hopped with me inside the tall French doors that lead from my back patio into the sun-room. Through the glass panes of the windows and skylight, we watched the storm roll in. This was no light shower. Torrential rain lashed at the glass. The walls trembled under the onslaught of the wind. On all sides we could see flashes of lightning, the crack of thunder following close behind. Though I knew we were safe inside the sun-room, the fury of the storm frightened my granddaughter so that I had to comfort her.

When the storm had passed, Dagmar and I stepped back out onto the patio. The air, fresh and clean, filled my lungs. The concrete under our feet was washed free of dust. Sunlight glistened from every blade of grass and leaf. Dagmar and I turned to search for a rainbow. Sure enough, there it was. Not just one rainbow, but the shimmering color palette of a full, bright double rainbow stretched from over my sister's house to touch down beyond my Amish neighbor's fields.

As we exclaimed over the beautiful sight, my thoughts went to the very first rainbow, as told in the biblical story of Noah in Genesis, the very first book of the Bible. After a worldwide deluge, God placed His rainbow in the clouds as a sign of His presence and as a covenant with Noah and all future descendants that never again would such a storm wipe humanity from the earth. I was struck by the realization that this beautiful double rainbow Dagmar and I were enjoying was a product of the very storm that had frightened her. Storms can sweep through with such violence and devastation. But storms also wash the earth clean. Storms bring life-giving moisture. And as a bonus, a gift from God for the delight of His children, storms produce rainbows. Without storms, there would be no rainbows.

And so it is with our lives. I did not choose the storms. I did not want the storms. And in the midst of gale and hurricane and tsunami, I could not see beyond simple survival, clinging to dear life in the fear of being swept under to drown. I sit now in my sun-room, surrounded by the loveliness of a storm-cleansed landscape, and I see the beauty God has wrought in my life and others' lives, not in spite of the storms, but because of them.

I look back to that sun-kissed, tranquil valley that was once my life, and I would not go back there if I could. Despite the pain and grief and an ocean of tears, I would not trade the experiences of these last years and all they have taught me. I have come through the storms to a spacious place of peace and surrender. "Amazing Grace," as the old song says, has taken on an entirely new meaning in my life. My heavenly Father's grace has brought me safe thus far, and it will carry me through every new tomorrow.

That is not to say more storms may not lie ahead. Even as I was finishing the writing of this book, I received the unwelcome news that after twelve years of remission, cancer has returned. The path that was stretching so straight and firm before me has now taken a sudden sharp curve. I don't know what lies around the bend. But I am not afraid. I've come to trust my life and my future to the God of both storms and rainbows.

So I sit here today in the aftermath of the tsunami that was October 2, 2006, facing yet one more storm on the horizon. As I look out through the rain-washed windows of my sun-room, it is not flooded fields and gray skies I see. It is the double rainbow. I feel so blessed. It is well with my soul.

I am at peace.
I am loved.
I am forgiven.

Terri Roberts has lived just south of Strasburg, Pennsylvania, for nearly three decades, and she and her husband, Chuck, are approaching the half-century mark in their marriage. She is a mother of four sons, a grandmother of eleven, including two step-grandchildren, and a member of Living Faith Church of God. She has survived serious illness and adheres, as a result, to an admirably rigorous diet.

Hers was a relatively quiet life until 2006, when an unthinkable tragedy in her community, a tragedy for which one of her beloved sons was responsible, propelled Terri into the public eye. At the finish of this book, Terri finds herself with another bump in the road, a diagnosis of stage four cancer. She describes herself as one who has walked through circumstances beyond her own ability to cope yet has found strength and even joy along the way. Hers is a message of God's grace given and received and the mountains it can move.

Terri travels the United States and the world, speaking about the Nickel Mines Amish school shooting, forgiveness, and hope. A documentary is being made on her life story. For more information or to contact Terri, visit her website: www.JoyThrough Adversity.com or send mail to PO Box 102, Strasburg, PA 17579.

Donations to provide for the continuing medical needs of the Amish schoolhouse shooting victims can be made to:

Community Care Center
PO Box 65
Intercourse, PA 17534-0065

or

Nickel Mines Accountability Committee
959 Georgetown Road
Paradise, PA 17562

———◇—◆—◇———

Terri's son Zach and a Swedish team are currently working on a documentary about the Amish school shooting titled *Hope*. For more information on the project, email Zach at Zachary@ mexico86.se.

———◇—◆—◇———

Having responded to some of the nation's most tragic school catastrophes, Cheri Lovre brings over thirty years' experience in exactly what schools need for crisis prevention and response. For more information about Crisis Management Institute, go to www.cmionline.com.